Are You Feeling a Little Finer, Miss Norene?

Are You Feeling a Little Finer, Miss Norene?

A Personal Account of My Year as a Volunteer Teacher in Namibia, Africa in 2009

Norene Hogle

AuthorHouse™
1663 Liberty Drive
Bloomington, IN 47403
www.authorhouse.com
Phone: 1-800-839-8640

First published by AuthorHouse 05/24/2011

ISBN: 978-1-4634-0121-4 (sc)
ISBN: 978-1-4634-0120-7 (hc)
ISBN: 978-1-4634-0122-1 (e)

Library of Congress Control Number: 2011907065

Printed in the United States of America

This book is printed on acid-free paper.

For the staff and learners of Heroes Private School in Ondangwa,
Namibia for accepting me and helping me to learn about
your people, customs and beauty of your country

CONTENTS

PREFACE

After having the opportunity of living and working in the developing nation of Namibia in Africa for the 2009 school year, I feel that I want to share it with others. People who are interested in education, traveling and learning about the culture and customs of those living in a third-world country will certainly want to read this book.

My choice was to go as a volunteer teacher to Namibia and my expectations were certainly fulfilled. Although I did experience a few setbacks, there wasn't anything I couldn't handle, but I did need the help of some very caring friends a few times. I would encourage persons of any age who have the time and the means and want to "give back" and/or "make a difference" to explore volunteer opportunities of which there is a multitude in the U.S. and all over the world. It will undoubtedly change your perspective on life and the world. Just explore the plethora of information on the websites.

ACKNOWLEDGEMENTS

I am grateful to my immediate family-Brad, Doug, Merrie, Racheal and to my very good friend Ron, for the love and support they gave me before, during and after my year in Namibia and to the many other relatives and friends who were interested in my venture and kept me in touch with the "outside" world.

To Brad Hogle for his help in editing the manuscript

To World Teach (www.worldteach.org) for accepting me into their program and giving me permission to use some of their information

To Google for the maps of Namibia and Africa

To *Lonely Planet* for some brief extracts from their Botswana and Namibia guide book

INTRODUCTION

Introduction--April 2008-December 2008

My adventure started in April of 2008 when I heard about the non-profit organization **World Teach** from a friend whose daughter was going to American Samoa as a volunteer teacher with this organization. She suggested that I investigate it on the internet which I did. About three days later I filled out the initial application online and sent it in. I had thought for several years of wanting to go to a foreign country as a volunteer teacher, particularly to Africa, since I had gone to Kenya in 1999 on a mission trip from our United Methodist Church to our "sister church" when I became fascinated with that part of the world. I had researched a bit on the internet with various organizations, but had not pursued anything in depth. When I found that going with World Teach was a one-year commitment, instruction is in English and the volunteer could choose the country which he/she preferred, this appealed to me.

World Teach, Inc. is a non-profit, non-governmental organization affiliated with the Center for International Development at Harvard University. It provides opportunities for individuals to make a meaningful contribution to international education by living and working as volunteer teachers in developing countries throughout Asia, Latin America, Africa, the Pacific Islands and Eastern Europe.

It recruits and places approximately 300 volunteers in overseas locations each year. There currently are teachers in countries including American Samoa, Chile, China, Costa Rica, Ecuador, Guyana, Kenya, Namibia, the Marshall Islands, Mongolia, South Africa and Uganda.

The four qualifications are to be 21 years of age, have a college degree (it doesn't matter what the degree is in), be a native English speaking person and have a desire to live and work in a developing country. There was no age limit except for going to China in which it was 65 years. I deemed that I was qualified to apply. The age limit has now changed, with 65 years being the limit for application. I was a little surprised that teaching experience was not a requirement to go abroad as a teacher, but there is a three-week orientation before going into the classroom. Apparently World Teach believes this is enough of a background.

My experience had been 31 years as a teacher here in the States and a few years abroad so this didn't concern me very much. Some of the initial application papers sent in were writing three essays mostly about experience and expectations about living and coping in a developing country, getting two character references, a resume` of past work experience and having an interview with two former World Teach volunteers living in Seattle (hence close to where I live north of Seattle) who had been in Namibia in 1996. At any rate, after sending in these items, I received a call from Cambridge, MA about mid-May saying that I had been accepted into the program and I was elated. I had told my family about all of this with the initial application so they wouldn't be shocked by the whole thing. Actually, I don't think they are surprised about anything that "Mom" does anymore. After being notified, I spent the next six months getting ready for the experience in different ways.

There were a number of other papers to fill out and send in including a notarized letter from the local Police Department which did a background check on me, photocopy of birth certificate, two copies of information on my passport, four passport photos, two photo copies of my Bachelor's degree, two copies of an updated TESL (Teaching English as a Second Language which I did at the local elementary school), transcript of college grades, copy of a recent physical health form signed by my doctor, getting various inoculations and medications applicable for Namibia, application for a Visa Work Permit to teach in Namibia, a Travel Plans form and, of course, the money which was about $6500 to go to Namibia. The charge for some of the other countries is less but I wanted to go to an African country, Namibia, as my first choice and Costa Rica in Central America was my second choice. I think the price depends upon how much the host country can contribute. When one goes as a volunteer worker, one pays the cost because it is the choice of the individual to do this service.

Since I own my town home here in Mukilteo, WA, I needed to make a decision about this. I decided not to rent it out, but just leave it vacant while I was gone. I have wonderful neighbors who said they would "keep an eye on it" and one of my sons lives nearby. He checked on it, as well, almost weekly. He was my CFO while I was gone and I made him a co-trustee of my Trust; he did a very fine job. He was in banking for several years so knows all about facts and figures. I trust my other son equally, as well, but since he lives seventy miles away, this was not convenient. Now it was a matter of waiting until I would be leaving for a year on December 29, 2008 for Washington, D.C. and then on to Johannesburg, South Africa, to Namibia and lastly to Ondangwa in the northern part of Namibia where I was assigned to teach.

The chapters in this book are taken from my daily journal writings and letters I sent back to my contacts from my home in Namibia. As it happened, I did send a communication almost monthly. I was able to buy an Internet connection for my laptop which I could use in my home. I was very grateful for this because it made for a quick connection with my family and friends in the States. I did use the regular airmail at times which took about three weeks each way so you can see email was so much quicker. Brad saved and printed off all the communications I sent home. I was able to save a lot of them as well after I established my internet.

My hope is that you will enjoy reading this account. Although I am not a professional writer I've done quite a bit of writing just for my own personal enjoyment and use.

This whole experience is something I shall never forget and I feel that I have taken a piece of Africa with me in my heart or perhaps I have left a piece of my heart there. I know that I gained much more than I gave.

Norene Hogle
March 2011

THE JOURNEY BEGINS

Chapter 1--December 29, 2008-January 4, 2009

On Monday, December 29, 2008, I left Mukilteo, WA for Dulles Airport in Washington, D.C. for my December 30th flight from there to Johannesburg, South Africa. Son, Brad, was able to take me to SeaTac Airport for which I was grateful. The Puget Sound area had had a heavy snowfall and freezing temperature for about two weeks which was highly unusual for this area. Consequently there was a lot of snow and ice everywhere which made driving conditions difficult, something to which we are not accustomed here. I had two heavy suitcases, the carry-on bag and my laptop. We were cautioned about limiting our baggage for our year away from home by our field director in Namibia because of weight limitations and possible extra fees, but it seems that no one in the group paid much attention to this; I didn't have to pay anything extra but some did.

The World Teach group heading for Namibia met at Dulles Airport on Tuesday afternoon at the check-in area to meet each other, receive some documents and participate in some get-acquainted games. Most of our group of thirty one was there although some had made their own way to Africa and would meet us later in Namibia. The Dulles-Johannesburg flight was good but quite long, about fifteen hours. It did seem strange to have full meals and drinks served without having to pay for anything as opposed to flights in the United States.

At Johannesburg Tambo Airport we were met by our field director, Jocie from whom we had received many letters over the last few months and were taken to a nice hotel near the airport. This was New Year's Eve

Day. My roommate was Evelyn and we would be "roomies" for the rest of the time when we were not in our villages where we taught. She was a "senior" like I am. There were five seniors in our group: Bill and Linda, a couple from New England, Vic from Australia, Evelyn and I; the rest were in their 20's and 30's, some of which had just graduated from college. There were several who had taught school at various levels at one time or another. Most were from the U.S., three from Canada, two Australians, and one delightful young lady from Trinidad. After a rather late dinner, Evelyn and I went to bed but the younger folk did stay up to see the New Year in from the front door of the hotel. We were warned not to leave the hotel even for a walk because of the possibility of being accosted. There was a rather healthy thunder storm that night, the first of what would be many during the summer months.

The next day we boarded the bus for the short ride to the airport to take the flight to Windhoek, Namibia. There was a lot of confusion about getting the baggage weighed for the charge of being over the limit for the flight to Windhoek because most of us had over 44 pounds (20 kilos). Going to Johannesburg, there was no problem because each passenger was allowed two bags of 20 kilos each. We were in line for a long time because each agent could process only one passenger at a time but we did finally get through with only a little time to spare even though we allowed three hours to check in. The overage charge was quite steep, so World Teach did pick up the cost up to $80 U.S. but some were still over the amount. Later on we learned that the six people, who had gone on an earlier flight, because we were too many to all go on the later flight, went through the check-in process very quickly and weren't charged at all for excess baggage.

The Backpackers Unite (BPU) where we stayed while in Windhoek was pretty nice as far as hostels go. Evelyn and I had a double room with shower and toilet attached but the "younger folk" were in rooms with bunk beds with the bathroom down the hall. Maybe World Teach deferred to our ages? There was a group kitchen and living room that everyone staying in the facility shared. There were a few other guests but our group occupied the majority of the hostel. It had a swimming pool which was used by some especially in the afternoons when the weather was quite warm. The meeting room where we had our orientation sessions, was outside and open, but had a roof. It was a very noisy place with the sound of all the traffic passing by and sometimes the breezes were strong enough to blow the charts hither and yon.

The hostel was about a mile's walk down to the center of the city and we did have a chance almost every day to go there for an hour or more. Everyone, it seemed was interested in going to the internet café to check on e-mail particularly and do a little shopping. Many of the streets in this part of the city had names of German composers such as Mozart, Beethoven, Grieg and Brahms with the German name for street (*strasse*).

The downtown part of Windhoek has a very modern infrastructure where one can get almost anything that is found in many cities. The population is 240,000 but two-thirds of the people (160,000) live in a section called Katutura which is a very poor area with poor housing and health conditions. Some of the areas of the city are the result of the apartheid movement which happened here as in South Africa when that country had control of Namibia. We did enjoy our forays downtown.

Our field director, Jocie, said she had arranged for a special treat for Saturday night--a Herero traditional dinner. We boarded the bus an hour late, because the bus driver who was invited arrived without the bus. He had been invited but didn't know he was supposed to bring the bus for the thirty-plus people. He was dressed "to the nines"--a very handsome figure. Jocie drove him to the bus barn which was closed for the night. I don't know what transpired there, but he did finally come back with the bus and drove to the Herero part of town. It was kind of a rundown neighborhood. At any rate, the chef and her assistant came out and greeted each one of us with a hug and kiss on both cheeks.

Then we were shown to the outside dining area which was very attractive with an African motif, naturally. It was a very balmy evening so perfect for an outside meal. There were three different seating areas. The assistant told us about the many accomplishments of the chef (I don't think she spoke English) and showed a diploma and pointed out the badge on her chef's uniform while she smiled and bowed. We had some drinks and took many photos then were told the meal was ready. The food was laid out buffet style in the kitchen. There were four meats, including pork chops, lamb chops, goat and some kind of organ meat, then potatoes, a tossed salad and potato salad. On a special tray were three goats' heads skinned and roasted with the eyeballs still in them. This was the favored part, apparently. After settling down to eat this famous cook's meal, we found that we could not cut, chew or swallow any of the meat because it was so well done that it was tough and impossible to eat. It was seasoned well. This is when I found that the piece of meat I could cut was tongue, I think, but I'm not a big fan of that particular cut of meat.

A little later a goat's head was brought out and placed on each table.

Bill, at our table, had the honor of cutting this but it was just as tough as the other meat had been. Dessert was a small dip of ice cream which was good and for the last course was some sour goat's milk. About three tablespoonfuls were put in each cup. Since I could smell it from four feet away, I declined to take any. We thanked them profusely for the meal but they couldn't have helped but see that hardly any of the meat had been eaten. After this meal some of us thought, if this is Namibia's finest chef, we weren't looking forward to the food here; however I must say that I did have some very fine meals later on in my stay in the country. It was an experience to remember-or perhaps forget. I guess this was just the Herero style of cooking. They must have very strong teeth. When we returned back to the hostel, some of the people immediately went to the kitchen to make peanut butter sandwiches.

TRAVELING NORTH FOR PRACTICE TEACHING

Chapter 2--January 5-January 17

The next morning, after the Herero dinner, we boarded the bus to travel up north to a school near the Angolan border where we would do our practice teaching. You will remember that the majority of our group had never had experience in teaching and after three days of orientation and a pile of literature about it, were going into a classroom to actually teach. The drive to the village where the boarding school was took about eleven hours with a few stops. The scenery was very interesting since the desert and veldt country was green with grasses, low bushes and smaller trees due to recent rains. It was warm on the bus but bearable and not too uncomfortable.

The towns were neat and rather tidy until we crossed the "Red Line". Quoting from the Lonely Planet guidebook: this is where "the Animal Disease Control Checkpoint veterinary control fence is separating the commercial cattle ranches of the south from the communal subsistence lands to the north. The fence bars the north-south movement of animals as a precaution against foot and mouth disease and rinderpest, and animals bred north of this line may not be sold to the south or exported to overseas markets. As a result, the Red Line also marks the effective boundary between the developed and developing world. The landscape south of the line is characterized by a dry scrubby (open grassland) of vast ranches, which are home only to cattle and a few scattered ranchers. However, north of the Animal Disease Control Checkpoint, travelers enter a landscape of dense bush, baobob trees, mopane scrub and small *kraals* (farms) where the majority of individuals struggle to maintain subsistence lifestyles."

Namibian *kraals* began to appear; these are the pole-stick fenced-in circles with round thatched-roofed huts belonging to an extended family. The fences keep wild animals out and the livestock in and safe at night. Occasionally there is a stucco building in the compound and in one, I saw a car parked outside. The young people were driving their herds of cattle and goats that had been out all day grazing back to the family home for the night. Donkeys are the beast of burden here and one can see carts and "family wagons" being pulled by these animals. There were more and more termite hills appearing the farther north we went; the largest ones were probably six or seven feet high. There are even larger ones than these. When we went through the village of Ondangwa, where I was assigned, Jocie pointed out "my" school, Heroes Private School, and said that it is known as one of the "rich" schools.

It was dark when we arrived at the boarding school where we were for five days. Some cattle and donkeys inhabit the school grounds so one needs to watch for their "deposits". It was tricky wheeling our bags over the sand to the dorms trying to avoid the cow piles in the dark. I don't know how old this school is but it is in a state of disrepair. The bathrooms would be a plumber's nightmare, I should think. Two of the twelve faucets at the sinks had water and one of them had no drainpipe so the water just went to the floor and eventually out the doorway. Two of the twelve toilets were flushable with the ten others having unflushed products in them. You can imagine the smell! Eight of the showers worked, which was good. There was no hot water which is not unusual, but it wasn't bad taking a shower, rather like jumping into a cold swimming pool and getting used to the water. The men were supposed to use the bathroom facilities in the neighboring dorm but the water was off there, so we all used the same one. If anyone had any modesty before all of this, they certainly didn't afterwards. The majority of the laundry tubs in another building DID have water which was good. Clothes dry quickly because of the dry heat. One of the returning teachers who was at another secondary school said these conditions are pretty much the norm. I can't imagine how everything works out when the dorm is full with 140 secondary learners during the regular school year.

The regular school year had not yet started, so our learners (they are called learners here rather than students or pupils) were volunteers. Each of us was paired with another person in our group for our practice teaching experience. My teaching partner, Lindsey, a delightfully young lady fresh out of college and very eager to start teaching, and I were to teach English to grades 5-7. What we got were learners 4 years old who had never been to school, with one still in diapers, to grade 4, so we had to be quite creative especially without any materials to speak of. There were twelve learners which we separated into two groups for the last two days. We only taught for two hours a day for four days. The learners were from kindergarten through grade 10. One of the young men in our group decided to leave the program and go back home, which he did before the week was over. He had traveled to other countries and had taught English in Peru recently but this wasn't his "cup of tea" apparently.

Our cooking and cleanup was done by committee and this worked out pretty well. Everyone in the group was willing to "pitch in" and do anything that needed to be done. One has to be of this mind when volunteering in a developing country. The kitchen in the dorm where we were had no power so we had to use the one in another dorm. One problem was that the fridge and oven hotplate could not be plugged in at the same time without blowing a fuse. The first "cooking committee" got it all worked out that night we arrived, so we had dinner about 9:00 PM. My group was cleanup on the last night; the water went off about 6:00 PM. The dinner group was able to do their job but there wasn't enough water to do the dishes which we needed to do because of leaving the next morning. Two of the returning teachers who were with us knew of some well faucets outside the school complex in the fields and did find one with water about a quarter of a mile away, so we carried the dishes, pots, etc. out there and washed them by flashlight. This was another "character building" experience.

Our accommodations were in one of the dorms, as I mentioned before; there were fourteen bunk beds in each room. My roommate, Evelyn, and I were in with the married senior couple, Bill and Linda, but each of us had plenty of room. The others were about six to a room. A number of us had bedbug bites about the second day probably from the filthy mats on the bunks but they didn't hurt or itch and started going away after we left the place. There were cows and donkeys on the grounds as I said before and one group of cattle seemed to like to spend most of the day lying in the shade of one of the very large trees near the buildings.

One afternoon a number of us went to a nearby *shebeen*/bar for a cool drink and to relax and talk. It was fun mingling with the local people although I didn't enjoy the very loud music very much but this always seems to be a "given" at any gathering. The weather was delightfully cool in the morning but became increasingly warmer during the day and didn't cool down very much at night.

After leaving this place, which no one shed any tears over, and going back to Windhoek to wrap up the orientation, we did drive through Etosha National Park which is the largest game park in Namibia. This was the first opportunity to see some "African" animals but we didn't have time to go off the main road to the water holes where more animals gather. Some of the animals spotted included springbok and other "deer type" animals, wildebeest, zebra, two elephants, giraffe and a lion. It was a pleasant interlude for us but was very hot in the afternoon. A few of us did plan to go back a few weeks later for further exploration since the park was only about a two and a half hour drive from the schools where we would be teaching.

The hostel in Tsumeb was very nice. The plan was to stay one night but Bill was very ill from his diabetic condition and went to a local hospital, so we were there for two nights so we had some of our next orientation sessions here. We did go to a very nice restaurant one night and saw how the "non-hostelry/non-volunteer'" clientele dine. Tsumeb is below the Red Line and is a clean nicely laid-out city. We enjoyed our stay there and I would have opportunities to go back there later on in the year. Some kind of a mechanical problem had developed with the bus so another one was sent to replace it. It was really a "piece of work". The pavement was visible from part of the floor behind the driver's seat. It didn't seem that Bill would be comfortable riding all the way back to Windhoek in this bus so they rented a car and Vic drove them back. The bus did stop at the hospital so we did get to see Bill and Linda before we left Tsumeb.

Back in Windhoek at BPU the orientation sessions continued. We did enjoy being back in Windhoek but I think most of us were anxious to get to our schools and start working. A celebration *braai* (barbeque) was planned for our last night, Friday night, before going to our teaching posts the next day; people were looking forward to this. Some of us went to the *Bottle Store* (like a convenience store) about three blocks away to buy some snacks and drinks for the *braai* and the trip next day.

Evelyn and I decided to skip the last hour of our language class which was a total waste of time, according to our thinking, and go to the Bottle Store. W-e-l-l this turned out to be a BIG mistake. As we were walking back to the hostel with our purchases and were about a half block from BPU, two young men came running up behind us and mugged us. There was no one else around unfortunately in this residential area which is probably why they chose to do this at this time. One of the men reached into my pants pocket and grabbed my wallet while the other was trying to yank Evelyn's shoulder bag from her. She resisted so he drug her down to the street and dragged her along to wrest it from her. Her arms and legs were scraped on the pavement resulting in bleeding; she, also, hurt her knee. I wasn't hurt. We started running after them crying and screaming; naturally we couldn't keep up with them.

When we got to the next street, a man out in front of his house asked what had happened and when I told him, he jumped in his car to see if he could catch them on the next street. When he returned he said he didn't see them but some people standing on that street said they saw two young men running who then jumped into a taxi, so they were gone. Some other people appeared and offered help but there was nothing anyone could do at that point. Evelyn meanwhile had turned back to the hostel because she was bleeding rather badly. The man walked me back and advised me to put everything in a pocket, under my clothing and beware of my surroundings at all times. We had been cautioned about this, as well. I did learn a lesson from this "character building" experience, one I wish had not happened. He expressed his sorrow that this incident had occurred. The Namibian people, the honest ones which is most of the population as in any country, do not like to see this happen to anyone. While we were still walking back, some of the group came from the hostel to see how I was, because Evelyn had returned before to get help and tell them what had happened. They were relieved that I had not been hurt.

My credit and debit cards, World Teach work permit and some Namibian money were in my wallet, so I didn't lose a great deal. I always carry my passport, most of my cash, travelers checks and other documents in my money belt around my waist under my clothing when traveling. Evelyn had put "everything" in her shoulder bag for the drive up north the next day so lost many things. In reviewing all of this later in my mind, I know those two "jerks" had been standing a little bit away from us in the store when we paid for our purchases and put our money away. They were, also, walking down the middle of the street as we were walking along the path by the street. When we turned into our street, there was no one around so this is when they decided to make their move. We heard a few months later that the same situation had occurred in the exact same place - near the Bottle Store-but this time there was a policeman on the scene. When he told the men to stop, they jumped into a waiting taxi and the policeman shot one of the men in the taxi killing him. It seems taxi drivers are "in" on some of these robberies.

I will say here that our young colleagues and Jocie, field director, got on their laptops and cell phones to help us out by calling family members and getting the phone numbers of the banks where our credit cards came from, plus comforting us. They were very kind and considerate to their older compadres. My son received a call at 6:45 on a Friday morning as he was getting ready to go to work, saying his mother had been mugged but was unhurt. I had asked one of the young people, Katie, to talk to him to take care of reporting my cards being stolen. It was hard for me to hear on the cell phone because of the confusion, my hearing, the sheer noise of everyone being in the living room/ kitchen of the hostel awaiting the braai and a thunder and lightning storm occurring outside. Someone had bandaged up Evelyn's scrapes and then Chris and Chloe, our young couple from Canada who owned a car, took Evelyn to the hospital for her to get help there. They came back a few hours later with her being bandaged up quite well but fortunately she had no broken bones. She was in pain that night; Chris and Chloe took her back to the hospital the next morning for a review before they left to drive up north. They were very generous in giving people rides in their car all through the year. Evelyn had to stay behind for four days to get checked at the hospital again and to apply for a new passport at the American Embassy in Windhoek. I offered to stay with her but she said this was not necessary. Mr. Kapia, the owner of my school in Ondangwa, drove her up in his car four days later because he was at their home in Windhoek and had been asked to do this. Mr. and Mrs./Dr. Kapia are very kind generous people.

The next morning, Saturday January 17, most of the World Teach Group left by bus, van, or car for our teaching assignments. Since the majority of the group was going to the north central part, Jocie had ordered a full-size bus but what came was a fifteen passenger small bus which didn't seem big enough for us and our entire baggage. She argued with the driver and tried to get a bigger vehicle but to no avail. At first he said he would take all of the passengers and part of the luggage with the rest to be delivered later, but she said, "No" to this idea, I think not knowing if the "second shipment" would arrive. In the end everything went; we were stacked in like cordwood with very creative packing. The ride was about eight hours to Ondangwa, where my school was, the first stop. It was rather warm and we went through a few very heavy storms along the way but did arrive safely. It was interesting seeing the changing scenery along the way once again.

Several people helped unload my things plus Vic's (from Australia) which I was going to store for him for a few days. He had bought a motorcycle in Windhoek and was riding it up north so couldn't take his luggage with him on the bike. He is a rock and gem collector so there were a few very heavy boxes of rocks. I didn't attempt to pick those up. The cleaning crew was in the apartment when we arrived along with Dr./Mrs. Maria Kapia who was directing the operation. Directly after the bus left, I discovered that I didn't have my smallest bag which contained all of my medications plus other items. I went out across the yard screaming and flailing my arms to try to get someone's attention; thankfully someone did see me and the bus stopped. It was already out on the Main Road going north. We couldn't find my bag; they thought it was back at the apartment and I had just missed seeing it but I knew it wasn't there! The bus driver did say that if it was on the bus, he would bring it back to me after he deposited everyone else at their places and this is what did happen. He came back about two hours later. I was very grateful to have it back!

HEROES PRIVATE SCHOOL-GETTING ACQUAINTED

Chapter 3-January 2009

Heroes is a semi-private school which means, as I understand it, the owners provide most of the financial support, but the Ministry of Education supplies the copy books the learners use for the class work and activities and the school must follow certain guidelines, rules and procedures set up by the Ministry. The fee for each of these learners was $300 Namibian per month which is about $40 U.S. I arrived here on the 17th, school started on the 19th and I started teaching on the 21st.

On the first day of school, some 400 learners arrived bright and early. They lined up in straight lines for the assembly, according to their grade level, between the first two classroom buildings and listened quietly. One of the teachers led the assembly reading scripture, saying prayers then instructing them on the value of obtaining a good education. They heard this same message many times during the school year. Then Mr. Imwala, the school principal, addressed the group and introduced John Carlo and me, the new teachers on the staff.

All learners in every Namibian school wear school uniforms. I think this is the norm in most foreign countries. Heroes learners' uniforms are black trousers for the boys with white shirts; for the girls it is black skirts, jumpers, or trousers with white blouses. Shoes are black and socks are white. The shoes are to be neat and polished. This was a little hard to adhere to when there was a lot of water and mud around. Then in the drier times there is the sand with which to contend. There is a standard for hair, as well. Most of the boys wear their hair very short or closely cut. Most of the girls have braids or short hair. Any long hair must be tied down.

After the assembly was finished there was a staff meeting in the library, the first of many. I found immediately that I had difficulty understanding the Namibian "brand" of English, as I call it. All staff meetings begin the same way. The principal says, "Good morning, colleagues." Then often times after looking at his/her papers says, "We don't have much to discuss." Sometimes there was nothing on the agenda but it always seemed to take at least twenty minutes to discuss "not much or nothing". Mr. Imwala announced that he would be leaving at the end of the week to take a position in the circuit. Just one more note about staff meetings which were always held in the morning and many times were not finished before 8:00 AM starting time for the first period, so some of the 8th, 9th and 10th graders who wore blue shirts with "Perfect" pins were assigned to the classroom to monitor the classrooms. They were pretty good at classroom control.

At the end of this first meeting, the principal asked three of the teachers to stay for a bit longer. Since John Carlo and I had not been assigned to anything yet, we were there as well. Mr. Imwala asked each one in turn if he/she would take on the administrative position. Each one said, "No," because they wanted to keep their teaching position. He said he would tell the Circuit and perhaps they would find someone to fill the post. As it turned out one of the three did accept this responsibility. I don't know how this came about but Mrs. G. became the Acting Principal; I had the feeling that she was rather pushed into it, but I could be wrong. She was knowledgeable and did a good job. One disadvantage was that she was the main *Oshindongo* (the native language in this area) teacher and it soon became evident that she couldn't do both jobs so *Oshindongo* instruction went pretty much by the wayside for the rest of the year, however the learners did have to take the exam at the end of each term for that subject.

During the first two days there was a lot of confusion and noise in the whole school at times because of getting supplies, mostly the copy books and some text books, to the learners. Some of the teachers did receive the books they had ordered the previous year. John Carlo and I sat in the library for the first two days on very hard chairs studying the syllabi and scheme of work for the subjects we would be teaching. My assignment was teaching English and Natural Science and his was Computers and Math. He ended up teaching English and some non-promotional subjects although he was very knowledgeable in the former two. There was a very rigid system of goals for each term and, in turn, a precise assessment procedure. This was pointed out during our orientation with World Teach. I think the principal and staff were trying to figure out what to do with us. Finally one of the staff came to tell us that we could go to the staff room to wait for our assignments, that is, which grades we would teach and receive the times-table (schedule).

In the staff room, each teacher who was teaching subjects to grades 5 through 10 was assigned a table for his/her work space. Pre-grade (kindergarten) through grade 4 classes were self-contained. There were eleven of us in the room; it was comfortable but sometimes became very noisy with the teachers joking around and talking very loudly. They told me I needed to talk louder and I tried my best to do this.

My assignment was 5th and 7th grade Natural Science and 5th grade English, the only three classes which remained that way for the whole year. I found this did take all my time with writing lesson plans, marking copy books, making out and grading tests, filling out necessary data on the Continuous Assessment Forms and trying to keep ahead of the learners, although I think I could have handled another class. The learners began to speak English in the 1st grade at Heroes, so they knew how to read and write it fairly well but didn‘t know what a lot of the words meant, but it was difficult for me to understand their English as with the adults. Another thing is that when they answer a question, they speak very softly but I think they were improving in speaking “loudly” by the end of the year. I believe this is cultural trait because children approach adults rather humbly and quietly. If they were loud and assertive they would probably be punished. I did ask if they could understand my English and they replied in the affirmative but I don’t know if they really understood or just gave me the “expected” response as I’ve found to be the case in other cultures where I’ve been. Sometimes I asked them to spell a word for my understanding and if this didn’t work, the last resort was to write it on the chalkboard; THEN I understood. I spoke slowly as I did in my previous teaching because I found that going fast doesn’t work.

The classes were large with about 40 being the norm; there were 43 in the 7th grade so there was hardly any “wiggle room” in that class. Thirty seven were in the 5th grade. Perhaps three or four learners in each class had a text book their parents had bought them and they would share these with those sitting near them. I did have some student texts to go by and the science text followed the required curriculum and scheme of study so this made it easier for me to teach. None of the English texts did so we had to pick and choose and "grab some things out of a hat," so to speak. The Ministry of Education of Namibia is very strict about following the required curricula and apparently made frequent checks although none ever came to our school when I was there nor was I ever observed in the classroom or evaluated by <u>anyone</u> even though this is spelled out in the administrator's duties. The classroom teacher has to write a lot of material on the chalkboard for the learners to copy into their copy books. They have two copy books for each subject, one for daily copying and one for activities and homework. This follows the British and European system, I believe. With all of this writing by the teacher and copying by the learner there was hardly any time left for discussion of the lesson. I found that I had to fill every minute of the class period so things didn't get away from me. I did learn all the names of the 5th graders but not in grade 7. It was impossible to make a seating chart which I did a few times, but other teachers who came into the classroom rearranged the children to their liking. If I hadn't had the two student teachers in term 2 from the neighboring teacher's college who took over my science classes, I would have learned the 7th graders names. I made out "name plates" with each learner's name on a paper plate for them to have on their desks to hold up when they volunteered to answer a question; these were collected at the end of the period each day. This did work however the student teachers were not interested in using them; they preferred to point to each person for a response.

In March I received a class set of 20 English books which I had ordered for grade 5. This way two people could share a book and I didn't have to write as much on the chalkboard for them to copy. In term 2 which started in late May, I bought enough Science texts for both classes so two people could share one text. I had decided to do whatever would make my life easier in the classroom. I devised a way to keep track of all these books and never let any learner take one home, otherwise they would all have disappeared over time. Things had a way of fast disappearing and, of course, **no one** could ever explain how this happened.

The learners were not as eager to learn as I had anticipated; about one-third were really interested in cooperating and doing their best work, one-third were "so-so" and the last third seemed to be there for the social aspect. This last group liked to talk, be disruptive in class and not do the homework assignments which were a requirement. They never did anything "bad" so to speak. After a time I decided to do my best to help those who were really interested in getting an education. Although corporal punishment was allowed in the schools up to twenty years before, when Namibia became an independent country it was outlawed, although it is still practiced in some schools. Heroes does not allow this according to the Code of Conduct which was signed by every parent and learner in 2009, but some of the methods used to correct a learner by a few of the teachers I thought were worse than getting a few whacks on the backside. This was difficult for me to watch as it was meted out in the staff room mostly. My learners knew I wouldn't "beat them", as they called it, because I told them I don't believe in hitting anyone. I had no problem with grade 5 but some of the learners in grade 7 took advantage of my belief by not cooperating, it seemed to me. The comments in this paragraph are, of course, according to my observation and opinion.

During this first week sometime, Vic, my Australian friend who was teaching in another village about twenty-five kilometers north, came to collect his things I had been storing for him. He had hired a taxi to follow him down to my place to take all of his gear and left the motor bike for the time being at my home until the taxi would bring him back so he could ride the bike back to his home. His place was hard to find in the daytime, even with directions so almost impossible at night; he was living in a house at the back of a teachers' college. He went on to tell me about his trip up to his school on the day the rest of us came by bus. I mentioned before that we came through several thunderstorms during that trip. Well, Vic was on his motorcycle at the same time and got soaked several times. At one point he ran out of petrol and no one would stop to help him out in the pouring rain. Finally a farmer with a pickup truck did stop. They loaded the bike in the back of the truck but Vic had to sit on it with his feet on the floor to keep it from tipping over. So there he was bouncing along in the back of the truck astride the bike in the pouring rain going to get petrol. He did get to a station and got some fuel. That night he stopped at a very nice lodge, had a hot shower, a good meal and a nice bottle of wine, according to him. He asked someone on the staff to iron his clothes dry before he started out again the next morning. Of course, he got soaked all over again going through another storm. By the time he was telling me all of this, we were both laughing about the whole incident, but it wasn't funny at the time for him, as those things go.

MY HOME AWAY FROM HOME- MY LIVING QUARTERS

Chapter 4--January-February 2009

My living quarters were very nice. My place was behind the school and my neighbors were very kind. I had a kitchen/living room combination, a bathroom with a shower, and a bedroom all to myself. My next-door neighbors and I shared the same building which was a concrete block structure with a slanted corrugated metal roof; they all worked at the school as well. Mr. and Mrs. Caparros are Filipinos who immigrated to Africa some years ago, lived and taught in a few different countries and are now Namibian citizens. They both worked in the library. Rina lived with them along with her infant daughter, Sherrie, and the nanny; I don't know how she came to be with them; she was the computer teacher and helped me a lot with my cell phone which I didn't understand, plus it was out of minutes most of the time, but I really didn't have more than a few people that I cared to call. I did learn more about the cell phone and texting as the year went on from my younger colleagues.

Another volunteer teacher from the Philippines moved in with them, John Carlo who liked to be called Mr. Fox. He taught English mostly, plus a few non-promotional subjects at times. He was not with World Teach but was traveling around Africa for several months, visited here, met the Caparros, and asked for a teaching post from the owners of the school. He is very bright and I could understand him very well; he helped me with my laptop on a number of occasions. I gave it to him at the end of the school year. He said he graduated from the University in the Philippines in Criminology, worked in that for some time but it was very stressful so he decided to go into teaching. A few weeks later, Marissa moved in with them. She was hired to replace the lead Science teacher, Mr. David, early in February who took a leave to pursue professional advancement and direct workshops in the circuit to science teachers in the region. Marissa and I became very good friends even though she is much younger than I am.

Indoor plumbing, electricity and gas were furnished as part of the host school's responsibility in my contract. I had a four burner gas stove with a good oven and after about a month, Mrs. Kapia (the owner of the school along with her husband) had a new microwave installed in the apartment. She had asked me the day I arrived if I would like to have one. What a wonderful surprise! The fridge was quite large for one person and guests when I had them.

There was no hot water so I used the Shower in a Bag routine which worked quite well once I figured it out. Before this, I had been taking cold showers which weren't too bad because the weather was warm, but one does learn to do it quickly. The first time, with the Shower in a Bag, I filled it to its five gallon capacity and found that I couldn't lift it (weak Norene) so thereafter I settled on three gallons which was quite ample. At first I put it outside in the sun on one of the molded plastic chairs I had since there was no flat smooth surface to put the bag on, as instructed in the directions. Sometimes there was no sun, so after a time I ended up filling it two-thirds full with cold water and then putting in water heated in my electric pot for the other third. This worked well and was easier than carrying the whole thing outside and then carrying it back in. Bed linens, pillows, towels, mosquito netting for the bed, cooking and eating utensils, plates and dishes were furnished so you can see that I had a very good living situation. I had an electric fan which I used almost every day except in the winter. When it stopped working, I bought another one to replace it.

Laundry was done by hand and hung out on the line behind the house. It didn't take very long to dry unless a thunderstorm occurred. Later on in September/October when the weather was hotter and drier, things hung out dripping wet would be dry in two hours. I did ask the nanny next door to do my bed linens and towels because I didn't seem to have the strength to wring them out very well. She earned a little extra money this way; I didn't want to ask too much of her because she was busy with the baby; she was very sweet and kind. Since she spoke very little English, we did lot of gesturing and smiling.

Our rubbish was thrown into a big pit back of the house, as was the school's rubbish. Some men dug the pit out about three feet deep. Everything went in there including paper, cans, bottles, boxes and what have you. It was burned occasionally and when it became full almost to the top, it was covered with dirt and another pit was dug. This happened twice during the year I was there. There was garbage collection in town sometimes; this was taken to a garbage dump outside of town. I went by that once and it seemed to extend for a quarter of a mile. Quite a messy scene!

The school was on the septic system. The truck was supposed to come every three weeks to pump it out but they were never on schedule and had to be called each time. We knew it was past time when the pipes gurgled back into the shower when the toilet was flushed. The toilets from the school were on this as well. Only once did it really get smelly plus there was two inches of "guck" in the shower. This was on a Friday and fortunately I was going to be gone for the weekend. When I returned, things had been taken care of, to my pleasure.

Since this is a warm climate, the little "beasties" as I call them were ever present. There were always several black spiders living on the walls and ceilings. This didn't really bother me because I was told they were helpful creatures. The little green lizards and bigger black ones usually stayed outside or just ventured into the window sills. They eat mosquitoes, I believe. There were always ants but they could be controlled pretty well with the spray *DOOM* and white powder sprinkled in the doorways and on window sills. It is absolutely amazing at their power and resistance because they came in between the tiles in the floor and where the floor meets the walls of the house. Their telltale sign was little piles of sand on the floor and wall, some of which had not been there the day before.

Cooking was very simple as it is back home and I did have nutritious foods. I took my lunch to school even though the school was only forty yards away. I had the same thing every day which made it simple: a meat or cheese sandwich, an apple and a small piece of banana or madeira bread and, of course, a bottle of water. I almost became a vegetarian because it was easier, although I did fix chicken quite often.

There was a large space between the front door and the floor. As one of my brothers-in-law always said, "It's big enough to throw a cat under." When the rains came, which was very frequently during those first few months, I put two large bath towels at my front door and then wrung them out each time and hung them out on the line to dry in preparation for the next storm which came almost daily. I didn't really mind the storms as long as I was inside and it was rather pleasant at night hearing the rain on the metal roof, that is until there was about a foot of water over much of the school grounds.

ANOTHER VISIT TO ETOSHA NATIONAL PARK

Chapter 5-Early February, 2009

During the first weekend of February, four of us went to Etosha National Park which is the biggest and best of the parks in Namibia; this was a nice respite. It was about a two and a half hour drive from Ondangwa. We looked forward to our weekends as most working people do. Vic, the Australian fellow, rented a van so we had plenty of space and this vehicle was able to make it through the numerous puddles which were on the roads in the park. Evelyn, the other lady who taught at a secondary school in Ondangwa, Vic's housemate Shinya from Japan and I made up the group. Shinya was with a group from Japan who are in an organization like our Peace Corps and he was going home in March after being here for two years. He wanted to visit Etosha one last time; he had been there the year before when his family had come to visit him.

On this trip, we did not see any elephants, white rhinos, cheetahs, or lions but we did see a number of other animals including springboks, kudus, zebras, oricks, giraffes, impalas, ostriches, weaver birds, cory buster and storks. It had been raining here a lot with some areas being flooded so the animals had a lot of vegetation and water without gathering at the waterholes for food and water. A helicopter pilot from the Wildlife Organization who was there flying over to look at the park said he did see those animals we didn't see but they weren't traveling in groups. We spent the day driving all around this very large park then drove a little south to a very nice lodge with the African motif, of course. We enjoyed being in nice furnishings, having a warm shower, and a very nice dinner including kudu steak and springbok shepherd's pie plus a number of other items from the buffet.

The next morning after a delicious breakfast we headed back to the park for another game drive but found that because of the heavy rain the night before even the parking lot had several inches of water in some places. Vic didn't want to chance going through even deeper puddles (some of them were like ponds) so decided to head back to Ondangwa on the major highway making a few stops along the way. Vic knew of a rock and mineral shop in one of the smaller towns so we spent some time there. He has quite a collection of these things and wanted to talk to the owner to see if he could get some more. He was able to order some "gem" rocks from the owner that he would pick up later. He seemed very pleased with his transaction. The owners are German people from South Africa so they spent quite a bit of time speaking in Afrikaans. Evelyn bought a pair of earrings, Shinya bought some rose stones to take back to his friends in Japan and I bought nothing.

Vic was born in Zambia (Rhodesia, at that time) and lived in South Africa for a number of years before emigrating to Australia. He had spent time in Namibia a few years ago as an engineer down in the diamond mines area in the southern part of the country. He was familiar with the roads, driving on the left side of the road and using the driving mechanism being on the right side of the car. Evelyn and I were thinking of other trips we could take in this northern part of Namibia with Vic as our hired driver with a rented car although we didn't tell him this, but we knew he would be amenable to the idea. However this did not materialize because Vic decided to go back home to Australia about mid-March.

THE VILLAGE OF ONDANGWA

Chapter 6

Ondangwa is typical of the towns up in the northern part of the country, I believe. There are many shops along the streets, most of which are a cement brick type structure with flat roofs. There are many hair salons and bars/ *shebeens* lining both sides of the streets, some of which look to be about 8 feet square. There are *shebeens* in every town, village and even out in the country. Most of the women and girls have the many braids so apparently there is a lot of business for the salons. Many wear hair extensions, I learned, and these are braided into their existing hair. Sometimes their own hair is very short so I didn't see how the extensions could be attached, but they were. At school some of the learners and teachers would have a completely different hairdo from one day to the next. It took me a while to figure out what was going on.

The main street running through Ondangwa is called Main Road, an apt name, and is on the main highway from Windhoek to Angola. The town is very long; we were told that people didn't want to build very far from the main street for fear of people breaking into their homes to steal. The side streets do extend away from Main Road for a few blocks. Streets do have names but very few are signposted. My learners did tell me this. I found out a lot of information about living in general from their talking and writings. I asked them a lot of general type questions. When asking for directions the answers were rather vague and confusing. The village people, of course, knew where they were going so didn't need to know street names.

There were some open markets every day in the village with groups of women sitting in the shade of the spreading branches of the trees. It was a time to socialize, as well as making some money for their families. There were always individual persons, mostly women, sitting by the streets or roadside with some fruits, vegetables, candies, small artifacts and/or snacks for sale. Most had a small child sitting by them or a baby strapped to their back. Each person or small group seemed to have their own spot every day although the places didn't seem to be marked off. One could get almost anything thought of at these markets such as vegetables, fruits, snacks, clothing, handbags, shoes, blankets, sweets, cooked sausages, chicken and fish, breads of different kinds, grains, flour, radios, sunglasses, Avon products, makeup, lotions, creams, and homemade and manufactured crafts. You name it and it was probably there somewhere.

The food stores (super markets) have almost everything there is in the U.S. but not the variety, so I ate the same things I do at home these being healthy food, not fast food or TV dinners. There were two sizeable grocery stores in town, Shoprite and Pic and Pay, plus some other smaller food stores. There were a few lower scale stores that sold items including clothing, shoes, household goods, and hardware. There are a number of what are called "China stores" which sell a great variety of lower quality merchandise. We thought the name came possibly from the fact that almost everything comes from China. Many of these stores have the word CHEAP in the name of the store such as The Cheap Store, The Cheapest Store, and Cheap China Store. Most seemed to be run by Namibians although I did see a few Chinese operating the stores.

There were always guards inside and outside the stores and banks. At the stores, the guards went through the bags containing one's purchases and checked them against the sales slip. It wasn't just a cursory check as I've experienced at COSTCO. Children were patted down as they were leaving the store. I did notice at Shoprite, the store where I did most of my grocery shopping, the guards weren't as intense as they had been at the beginning of the year and were usually quite friendly. I would like to think they had more trust in me as time went on.

Mr. Caparros went up town almost every afternoon after school was out and offered to give me a ride back if we met and I had more things than I could carry. Usually I would take a taxi home with my purchases. It cost $7.50 Nam. (80 cents U.S.) for a taxi ride any place in town. It was about a twenty minute walk to the center of town which I enjoyed. I usually walked with some of my learners who were walking (or *footing* as they called it) to their homes after the school day was over. I enjoyed having conversations with them because I got to know them better in a casual way and I hoped they saw me as a "real person" not just their teacher in the classroom. I learned early on after the mugging incident that I couldn't carry a camera, wear a fanny pack and if I wore a backpack I had it on the front of me or it might be grabbed. They won't take bags of groceries but anything of value that can be sold is "fair game". Unemployment is over 20% so theft is high, especially by young men. This is not to say that all young men are thieves but they seem to be the ones who do this mostly.

There were a number of schools in this village judging from all the different school uniforms I saw when I was in the central part of town and seeing children walking by my home in the morning and afternoon. Since Namibians are a highly Christian group, there were a number of churches from rather small to very large. The predominant church is the Lutheran because of the German influence when they ruled this country although there were other denominations of Christian churches. There were other businesses in town including funeral homes; furniture stores; medical clinics for doctors, dentists, and optometrists; car agencies; car and truck repair places; several banks; Avis car rental; pharmacies; internet café; office supply stores; and petrol stations.

There was nothing cultural in this town but there is a restored Finnish Mission, Nakambale Museum, several kilometers out of town. Evelyn and I went out there one Saturday to visit. It was founded in 1871 by Rev. Martri Rautanen. I felt the people had done a good job of displaying artifacts from the Ndonga Culture and the Finnish Mission history. I believe there is still somewhat of a connection between Finland and Namibia. We were the only two visitors there but we were given the whole tour.

The people here wear the same type of clothing as we wear in the U.S. and for some of the old and most of the young women, it seems the tighter the better it was for pants, skirts and tops. Two of our staff at times had the very plunging necklines which left very little to the imagination. Some of the older women do wear the "traditional" African attire which is a two-piece very colorful dress with the scarf around the head. The elderly women especially wear the "muumuu" type dresses and always the head scarf. Those dresses are cooler than the more traditional fitted type. We were advised by World Teach to dress modestly, but I do this anyway. The men wear trousers and shirts of different types as in this country. There was no "gangsta" type clothing that I noticed with the baggy pants with the crotch hanging down to the knees.

There were always taxis cruising around looking for passengers; one just had to raise a hand to flag them down and tell the driver where you wanted to go. If he was going that way you would get in; if not, you would just wait for another to come along. There was a "switch" point in the center of town just beyond the Shoprite store at the Shell station where taxis, combi vans and busses waited for passengers going north to the next towns or going south from Ondangwa. They liked to wait until their vehicle was filled before starting out. Everyone paid the same amount; it was not a "shared" fare situation so the drivers wanted to make as much money in one trip as they could. With the taxis, after about ten minutes, if it wasn't full they would leave hoping to pick up another passenger or two along the way. With the combi vans and busses, some going all the way to Windhoek, they might wait for several hours waiting to get more passengers before leaving. I don't know what the cost was to go to Windhoek but it certainly was a lot less than taking the plane, so if time was not a factor, I suppose one could wait all day. I did take a combi small bus to Tsumeb, a larger town about a two and a half hour drive south one time, and the cost was $120 Nam. We found that sometimes, even though a taxi driver said he knew where your destination was, he really didn't so he had to stop to ask people how to get there as he got closer. A number of them did not understand or speak English very well. There was not any public transportation in the northern part, to my knowledge, that ran on a regular schedule. There was a seatbelt law in Namibia which wasn't very well followed. In the taxis, the driver and passenger in the front seat were belted, but in the back seat it was hard to find the seatbelts; apparently they were pushed down behind the seats and sometimes there were more than three passengers in the back so there wouldn't be enough seatbelts anyway. Everyone survived pretty well, even with these conditions.

MORE ABOUT SCHOOL HAPPENINGS

Chapter 7

Each teacher's schedule or times table as it was called was different every day so there wasn't a regularly daily scheduled period at the same time for each subject. Once a week Math and English had a double period back to back. I would have liked this each day but with all the several subjects each learner had to take there wouldn't have been time to fit everything in. The learners took a number of different subjects having the basic ones each day but others just one, two, or three days a week, hence the varied schedule. The learners had a break in the morning from 10:40 to 11:10; this is when they ate the lunch they had brought. There was no government lunch program in Namibian schools-free, reduced or full payment. The older children in grades eight, nine and ten do not bring lunch or snacks to school generally. The general population seems to have a light breakfast of tea or coffee and porridge and then the main meal is in late afternoon or evening.

School started at 8:00 AM, but sometimes from my living room window I could see learners arriving before 7:00 AM because the parents drop them off before going to work, I suppose, or they were just told to leave the house early. The school day ended for the primary grades at 1:50 PM and for the upper grades at 3:30 PM except on Fridays when everyone was dismissed at 1:50 PM. There was a break in the afternoon from 1:50 to 2:30 PM and then from 2:30 to 3:30 PM is a study period in which some learners did study and others just "goofed" off. On Wednesdays the last hour was for "Clubs" including Science, Choir, Drama, Football, Math and one teacher, Mr. Fox, taught Karate; he is a Black Belt. Since I was one of the science teachers, this was my assignment as one of the directors of the Science Club. Mr. David, the lead science teacher whom I mentioned before, left the school two weeks after the term started so Marissa and I were in charge of the Science Fair Club. She nor I had any experience in this. We really kind of resented that he had "dumped this in our laps", but his consensus was that we were both experienced teachers so we could handle it. David had written a guide to follow but being "new to this game" we asked the learners who had participated before for directions in how to proceed. The learners had to select their topic for their investigation to be approved by David, so Marissa and I had to call to get the OK from him. Most of the time he wasn't available on his cell phone. We just decided we would do the best we could. There were the displays from previous years but none of the learners could choose a topic that had been done in the last several years, but it did give them an idea of how to proceed and it gave us, the leaders, directions of how to proceed. David did come back to Heroes about two weeks before the first of the Science Fair competitions started at the end of July. In the afternoon some children were still at school at 5:00 waiting for someone to pick them up. They arrived in the morning and left in the afternoon by taxi, vans, cars, pickup trucks and by *footing* as they call walking to any place.

The learners were responsible for sweeping the classrooms once or twice each day and mopping them on Friday. This was done by committee and everyone's name in the classroom was listed for one day each week. One thing I never could understand was that some children dropped papers and other things on the floor and never picked them up knowing full well they had to be cleaned up later. I tried to set a good example by picking up their things some times and always having my things neat and orderly, but most of them did not "get the point." I told them I had taught my own children and children in my classes to clean up their mess but it fell mostly on deaf ears. Some learners were assigned to mop up the water that came in at the doorways when it rained during school time. The brooms and mops deteriorated to a pretty deplorable state as the year went on but I suppose there was no money to buy new ones. In general, the learners didn't seem to take care of their things very well. In August, when a permanent principal was hired at Heroes, he tried to encourage the learners to take possession of their classroom and surroundings by making them as attractive as possible.

There were twenty-two people on the staff with the principal, secretary, teachers, librarian and two custodians. It was multi-ethnic in that there were, in addition to the Namibian teachers, two teachers from Kenya, three from Zimbabwe, four Filipinos and myself from the U.S. Most faculties in other schools did not have this variety, I learned, from talking to my World Teach colleagues. One of the two custodians seemed to spend most of her time talking to whomever wasn't busy at the moment. The man did quite a bit of "outside work." There was another man who was there part of the time, as well. Sand was always being carried into the classrooms even though the learners and teachers tried to kick it or stamp it off before entering the room. Sand was everywhere outside.

The teaching seemed to go about the same each day. I never really thought I was doing much to help them but perhaps time will tell. I think I had this feeling because the classes were so large and because of the lack of text books, I had to write everything on the chalkboard for them to copy so there was no time left to delve into their minds. As I wrote before, each learner had two copy books for each subject for note taking, activities, homework and taking tests and they could copy quite well; this was one time when everyone was very quiet, but their critical thinking was quite inadequate, almost non-existent. Some of my World Teach group said this was the way it was in their schools, as well. Everyday the copy books were stacked up on all the teachers' desks to be marked and handed back for the next day's work. I was very thorough in marking my books and recording grades because I wanted to see how each learner was progressing. Some of the other teachers didn't seem to record marks other than the required ones for the Continuous Assessment forms. I did have a vision that in a dream sometime I might be suffocating in a sea of copy books.

The thunder and lightning storms continued almost every day. I had to wade through some water to get to school but it was only about four inches deep. I wore my Teva sandals and then changed to other shoes when I got to the staff room. There were lots of little black tadpoles in all of the puddles and a little later they had changed to tiny frogs. The children were attracted to the water, of course, like all youngsters are. Most of them took off their shoes and socks when wading but some just tromped through shoes and all. The principal did make a change to the dress code by announcing they could wear "crocs" or "jelly-type" footware during the flooded season.

This is something about the grading system of the Namibian schools in grades 5 through 10. I do not know what pre-grade through grade four does and I didn't think to ask when I was there. In grades five through seven 80 to 100% is an **A**, 60 to 79 % is a **B**, 45 to 59 % is a **C**, 30 to 44% is a **D** and 29% and below is an **E** or failing, so 30% correct is a passing grade. I will confess that I was really surprised when I discovered this. In grades 8 through 10, 50% is the lowest passing grade; I don't know what it is for the secondary schools; i.e. grades 11 and 12.

The upper grades study a number of subjects including the basics: English, Math, Natural or Physical Science and Social Science. Then there were other subjects taught from one to three times a week including: Agriculture, Computer Science, Oshindongo which is the local ethnic language, P.E., Art and Religious and Moral Education. In grades 8 through 10, Business Math, Accounting, and Entrepreneurship were taught, so you can see there was a wide range of studies for these grades.

A unit of study about HIV/AIDS education was included in the scheme of work in all Natural and Physical Science, Social Studies and English courses in the upper grades; perhaps it was in other courses of study of which I was unaware. According to statistics over 20% of the Namibian population is affected with HIV or AIDS. I thought it was presented very well in the Natural Science that I taught so the learners do learn what they should and should not do in regards to this subject. All of my 5th graders knew that in order to prevent this disease, one should have only one partner, use protection when having sex, do not go with "sugar daddies or sugar mamas", do not come in contact with bodily fluids of another person, wear protective gloves if you need to help someone in the case of an accident where bodily fluids are present and do not share needles with anyone. I asked them when they started learning about HIV/AIDS and they replied, "in grade 1" so they begin to learn at an early age. It seems that following these measures is a different story. There is a stigma attached to someone having this disease so it is not discussed very much and the person and their families are ostracized to a point if it is found out, as I understand it. I did attend one discussion group at school in which the female teachers and girls of grades 9 and 10 participated. It was a quite open and informative meeting for the girls; a few of the them did participate by asking questions or giving observations; the learners seem reticent about responding to an adult as I have stated before. It was agreed there should be another meeting later on but I don't know if this did occur;

I never heard anything more about it. The male teachers and 9th and 10th grade boys had a discussion at the same time.

There are two very important exams that occur in the school life of the learners; one is at the end of grade 10 and the other occurs at the conclusion of grade 12. So much emphasis is put on passing these exams that we heard of suicides occurring because of failing the exam. This did not occur at Heroes to my knowledge. At our school, it was just the grade 10 exam. The heavy pressure started in term two in June, July and August and continued in term three. The exams were in the last two weeks of October, then the learners were out of school until the next year started in January. There were several staff meetings of teachers and parents of grade 10. The 10th grade staff decided to have all the grade 10 classes in term three during the first half of the day when it was cooler and the learners' minds were fresher; this meant that those of us who were teaching the other grades had to have our classes mostly during the second half of the day when it was getting hotter and minds were not as fresh. I didn't like this at all but there was nothing I/we could do about it. I noticed that the teacher who made up the times table (schedule) had most of his core classes, that were not in the tenth grade, before noontime. Those last two periods from 12:30 to 1:50 were a struggle at best, but when the temperature outside was between 95 and 100 degrees F with no breeze blowing in the afternoon, it was even more so. Well, we all survived. Learners who do not pass have an opportunity to go back to school the next year to study and retry the exam. I believe they had more than one chance to succeed if they took the initiative. There were tutoring situations available, as well. Some of these people were older than a regular learner would be and some had infant children but saw the value of an education and wanted to get to a higher level. Some learners just quit attending school after the 10th grade whether passing the exam or not but there were no jobs for them to go to work except on the family's small farm. The unemployment rate was over 20% so others, older young adults and older adults, had those jobs which a teenager might have in the U.S.

My knowledge regarding the 12th grade exam is limited since our school just went to grade 10. My friend, Evelyn who taught 11th and 12th grade English in a secondary school in Ondangwa said in her observation, grade 11 was almost a wasted year because many of the learners, at least in her school, did very little. There were no grades and no tests in that grade because the emphasis was on the end of the year exam in grade 12. One would think the learners would take the opportunity to start preparing for that all important exam a year ahead of time.

There were no substitute teachers for the school so if a teacher was absent because of illness, workshops, or personal leave, the learners were in the classroom without supervision. In the upper grades it would be just for the subject period of the absent teacher but in the lower grades it would be all day. This seemed to work out; of course, the learners became very noisy but there didn't seem to be any physical contact problems. At one time the 4th grade teacher was absent for a week for a workshop; when I walked by the classroom I asked where their teacher was (knowing full well she wouldn't be back for two more days) and was told, "She's coming". This was often the answer given when someone didn't arrive on time or was gone for a time: "She's/he's coming". This might be in a little while, tomorrow, the next day or sometime in the future. There were a few times when a teacher in the staff room did not go to his/her classroom when scheduled because he/she didn't feel like it or was doing something else or they would go late and come back early. It didn't happen often but it did occur. Such dedication!

THE RAINS KEPT COMING AND VALENTINE'S DAY WEEKEND

Chapter 8 --February 2009

The rains still kept coming almost daily and there were ponds (*oshanas*) in many places. We had several on the school grounds and they kept getting bigger all the time. The drainage system and culverts were not properly built in the first place, I was told, but this was an unusual year. I found out that the last time there was this much rainfall was in the late 1970's. The whole front of the school was flooded but so far all vehicles seemed to be able to go through the water; there are many that come morning and afternoon to deliver and fetch the learners. Of course, the children are attracted to the water and had been warned about playing and walking in it. The fact that some snakes had been seen in the pools inhibited some of them. I never saw any-just the little black tadpoles. A makeshift walkway was "built" at the edge of the water on one side for people to use as a walkway. It included planks, old doors, bricks, pieces of metal, wooden pallets and anything else that could be thrown down on the ground to be walked on. Of course it was a constant battle of building as things sank down into the mud and sand, but people coped pretty well with whatever came along. The older learners and some of the teachers did work on this building process when needed.

Our multi-purpose room was now home for five or six families who were flooded out. I had seen children playing there before and after school and on the weekends, when I thought the building was usually locked.

When I went in there one day, I saw areas cordoned off with one or two beds, a stove, refrigerator, a table, some shelving, and, of course, the TV. All the TVs were blaring away even though there weren't people in all of the units at that time. The rains were predicted to go through March. Of course, businesses suffered because people couldn't get to them and the supply trucks were not able to get through some areas. In 2008 some of the mines farther north and west were flooded out and there were no plans to reopen them.

On the weekend my friend Evelyn and I took a taxi (taxis are the usual mode of transportation) to the next larger town to do some shopping and just have a change of scenery. It cost us $12.00 Nam. each which is $1.20 U.S. for the 40 km ride. I bought a printer which I could plug into my laptop and it WORKED! With my non-mechanical ability I'm always happy when something does work that I install. It was on sale for $399 down from $519, I believe. It was small and I wanted something that I could carry easily. With the attachment to plug into the USB port, a ream of paper, and the tax, it came to about $500 but the exchange rate was almost 10 to 1 at that time, so it was about $50 U.S. I bought a table lamp which I had wanted so I didn't have to use night vision glasses to see over in the corner, where my desk is, after the sun goes down. So-o-o, I was pleased with my purchases.

We met Vic there at the Game store; he rode his motor cycle up from his home in a town south of there. We found a nice place to have a real cup of coffee. I prefer tea mostly but this was good. Evelyn liked her coffee but wasn't crazy about the Nescafe which is what was available mostly. There is ground coffee but she hadn't found any coffee makers at that point. Sometimes she said, "My kingdom for a real cup of coffee." (She did find a coffee maker later on that she used.) This place was run by a lady from South Africa; it was called "Lenore's" and had a wide variety of very nice items for the home mostly. Also, there was a hair salon so this is where we had a haircut every few months. There were Caucasian people there so I assumed Rita, the beautician, knew how to cut our hair. She said she loved to cut my hair and kept clipping away until I had to tell her to stop before she cut it all off.

After the shopping we went back to Vic's place for the afternoon, talked and looked at his gems through his microscope and pictures on his laptop. He always said that he was living in a *hole* but I didn't think it was that bad. It even had an enclosed back porch where they could hang their laundry instead of having to hang it outside where it might get rained on during this season. He said he had talked to his wife that morning and told her about his living conditions but she wasn't sympathetic with him. She told him he knew what he was getting into when he signed on.

He paints animals and his gems, the latter while looking through the microscope; he is multi-talented. It was all very interesting but I did get tired after a few hours. There are many, many rocks in his collection. Vic is a retired engineer from Brisbane, Australia and is working on his Master's degree in gemology or some kind of 'ology. This is just a hobby. He said he only has to find two more types of gemstones and then he'll have the degree. He was teaching computers to grades 5 through 7 at two different schools, but was not happy with his situation because of the number of students on each computer, usually four or five, who come once a week for a forty-minute period and their general lack of interest. This is the way it was in all the schools, judging from what I saw and heard. He had about 250 students altogether. Some are learning to turn the computer on while others know their way around everything and come in and go immediately to the internet which is not allowed. He was supposed to teach at a third school but someone broke into the school before the term started and stole all the computers and, of course, no one knows how this happened and when or if there will be any replacements.

Evelyn and I checked into a really nice hotel which Vic recommended, near where he lived where he had had dinner before and seen the hotel. This was Valentine's Day and the desk clerk made a big deal about the special Valentine's dinner they were serving that night. I will add here that there was "Valentine excitement" at the school the day before with the learners making and giving valentines to their friends. I received some, as well. I hadn't thought of them even knowing about Valentine's Day. It was nice to relax by the pool while having a drink. The air was very pleasant because there was a big storm brewing so there was a cool balmy breeze. The Valentine's special was very good. I had a prawn appetizer with pineapple sauce and the main course was Kingklip fish. It was a very delicious mild white fish and the veggies were al dente. Vic had this plus calamari which was done to perfection. It was very tender. We were the first there around 7:00 PM and last to leave after 10:00. Vic took off on his motor cycle; I don't know if he got caught in a storm or not. The dining room was filled and there were a number of high school aged kids out on the patio. They were there the next morning when we had our breakfast. Maybe they were on a field trip?

Staying in a hotel and being in a room with a shower or bath that had hot water was really a highlight for us. Then being able to have a nice meal that we didn't have to fix was always another pleasure. Everything is relative, of course. Also, we didn't have to "fight" the little insect beasties at night as in our own homes by closing all the windows and being very warm or leaving the windows open for a breeze and having the insects. We did always sleep under the mosquito net at home. We were in a malaria-area which is in just the northern part of Namibia. The rest of the country is malaria-free. The mosquitoes apparently don't like the hot dry desert and veld country which most of the countryside is.

Teaching remained about the same throughout the year. I think my frustrations were not with what I was teaching and the lack of some basic materials because I could "wing it" pretty well when I had to, but it was with the attitude of most of the learners. Some people from home did offer to send things but this wasn't necessary because the materials were there; there just wasn't the money in the school budget for them and postage is very expensive to send something from overseas. Namibia prints their own texts which are about this country and seem quite good; it is just that there isn't enough money to furnish each student with a text or even a set for half the class and most of the parents do not have the money to buy books for their children. I did state earlier what I did to alleviate this situation.

On a Friday night I had my first overnight guests other than Evelyn, who was there often on the weekend, or I was at her place. The two of us getting together was our "big social event" of the week being at one or the other's home or getting together on a Saturday some place in the town. Two of my young World Teach colleagues called about 9:00 PM asking if they could "crash" at my place for the night. They had been hitchhiking from their schools farther north and it had taken them longer than planned to get to a destination south of here. I never did understand where they were going. About fifteen minutes later when I looked out the window of my living room, I saw two flashlights beaming down the path to the back of the school. I did have room and a futon couch in the living area plus a double mattress that the teacher who was there the year before had left. We did get to talking and I found that they were having the same problems that I was which was interesting to me because during orientation they were ready to tackle the world for which I give them credit and thought "the seniors" didn't seem to know what we talking about. Erica (and she was one of them who was very nice to me) told that she was in a very poor school and economically disadvantaged area. Our Field Director told us that the learners from those areas are more receptive to learning and better behaved. Erica found this not to be true; they don't pay attention anymore than my classes did, besides this, there was not enough classroom space so two classes were combined and she had fifty-seven in one class. Another class meets outside under a tree. It reminded me of the book I read, Three Cups of Tea by Greg Mortenson. I told Erica that her journal is going to be more interesting than mine. She says that she will write a book. I did enjoy having them and we had a lot of laughs and sighs about our problems and joys of being in Namibia as volunteers for this assignment.

The next morning they were off hitching again and wouldn't even have anything to eat or drink. A lot of the young people and the Namibians hitchhike but this is something I never did. I took a taxi, bus, plane, and if those weren't available, I stayed home. When hikers did hitch a ride, they would pay the driver an amount comparable to taking a taxi so it worked out well for both parties involved. Some of my colleagues who lived in more remote areas had to do this because there were no taxis available. Some even had to walk a few kilometers on a dirt or gravel road to get to a main road where there might be cars or trucks passing by which they could flag down. I never heard of any unfortunate incidents happening from this hitching

The couple who lived next door offered me rides up town a few times a week to do shopping, although I usually walked up there. I think they may have thought I was too old to be walking especially in the hot sun but I always wore my sunhat and I really enjoyed walking. Mrs. Caparros always used her umbrella, as do a lot of the Namibian women, as a shield from the sun. It's available when the rains come, as well. She used it walking from the library back to their home at the back of the school.

CHURCH, BANKING, GHOSTS, PAYDAY

Chapter 9--February-March, 2009

One of the teachers at school, Helvi, invited me to go with her and her family to her church on Sunday. It is an Evangelical Lutheran denomination. There are no United Methodist churches, of which I'm a member at home, in this town and very few in the country. Some of the teachers asked me if I was a Christian, if I had been born again and to which church I belong. The population is largely Lutheran. Several hundred people attend this church each Sunday. This Sunday there was a baptism first, which lasted about twenty minutes. One of the family members, I presume, had the video camera rolling throughout. The service is rather subdued which I like but I did have the opportunity later in the year to attend one of the churches that has the hand clapping, shouting, and where things are really rocking and rolling. This church had the usual–scriptures, lots of singing which I could follow along with because the language is phonetic even though I don't know what the words mean, prayers, sermon and announcements. The regular service lasts about two hours. Helvi told me when to sit, stand and kneel and translated a little bit and where the scripture is so I could follow along in my Bible.

The week later there was a prophet, so after the regular service her spokesman spoke and then she preached. She was very elderly and wore a thick white robe decorated with silver and lace. Her headdress was much the same. She must have been roasting in all of that clothing because it was very warm. She had a wooden cross attached to her cane. Helvi told me some of what she said but I did understand it myself that the Lord came to her on January 30 and told her of the floods and other devastating things that were to come, and then the really strong storms did happen right after that. She lives in Ondangwa and has been a prophetess for a long time. Helvi said that some people believe her and some don't; sometimes she is right and sometimes not. That service lasted about three hours.

One part of the service is when the offering is taken, of course. During this time all of the people go forth to the altar, row by row and two by two. I liked to watch this because I got to see everyone and what they were wearing. They really dress up for worship services. At the altar is a cloth covered basket with a slot in it, but one of the members is standing a little to the side taking offerings, as well, in an open basket. If someone doesn't have an offering of their own, they take something from that basket and put it in the covered basket and do a slight curtsey while putting in their donation. The women and girls curtsey many times in other situations as well and always when receiving anything in their hands. Most of the older ladies wore muumuu type dresses and a colorful scarf on their heads. I commented about this to Helvi and she said they wear the head covering because they have gray hair and don't want it to show; they don't want to "apply the color." Then she asked me if I applied the color; I told her I didn't. She was surprised then looked closely at my hair. I think she believed me then. Some people don't believe that my hair can be a natural red at my age but it is, for which I'm grateful.

On Friday I finally opened a bank account in the village with Bank Windhoek; I brought travelers checks with me for this purpose. This took about thirty minutes for the paperwork and then we waited thirty more minutes for the clerk's supervisor to OK it. She was busy with another client. When she finally came, it took her about a minute to approve it; I don't know why she couldn't have taken that short of time to do it earlier but there **is** a lot of waiting around time here. I had gone the previous Saturday arriving in the queue at 8:30 AM and was second in line for thirty minutes and then first in line for forty five minutes. One man at the other window was there when I arrived and was still there after I left. When the person taking care of him went into the back and brought out a half dozen very large ledgers, I thought he would be there for the rest of the day, maybe he was. I don't know what kind of business he had that took him that long. At any rate, I was finally helped by Archilene at the other window who made copies of all my documents but I had one missing so was told that I would have to come back, but I wouldn't have to stand in the queue the next time.

The missing item was a credit card sized work permit with my picture on it that was in my wallet which was stolen when I was mugged in Windhoek. A work permit was stamped in my passport stating that I was a volunteer teacher for the 2009 school year but apparently that was not sufficient. I had to get a letter from my principal stating that I was, indeed, a volunteer teacher at Heroes Private School which Mrs. Gulu did write for me on Monday. Then I had to wait until Friday to go back to the bank because we didn't get out of school until 3:30 PM on Monday through Thursday, and this is when the bank closes. On Friday we could leave at 2:00 PM; most of the staff was out of there very soon after including me. There are two doors one must go through to enter the bank; there is a guard inside and outside, (sometimes there are two in each place) with a gun that looked like a rifle to me (I do not know guns). You go in the first door when the light is green; it locks behind you and then you wait inside between the two doors until the light turns green for the second one. The inside guard makes the rounds inside through the main room, as well, very frequently.

My monthly stipend was N$2378 which was about US $237 in the beginning when the exchange rate was 10 to 1. It was supposed to cover food and basic supplies (I don't know what basic supplies means–maybe toothpaste, soap, etc.?). Of course, I didn't go into this for the money. I found out later from my Field Director that I was supposed to get N$2885 but I didn't quibble about the difference because my housing situation was very nice according to NAM standards and the people who owned the house and school, had been very considerate to me.

Evelyn, the World Teach volunteer who taught across town at a secondary school, and I went to a hotel for lunch. We were the only ones there but we had a nice luncheon and chat. We had been getting together each Saturday, as I have mentioned before, for our "social event" of the week. At this time she was recovering from her latest frightening experience. She was at the opening morning exercises at her school two weeks before on Monday when one of the 12th grade girls screamed and fainted because she saw a ghost, causing the whole assembly to go berserk with screaming and running all around. In the melee, Evelyn was knocked down and stepped on. She thinks it might have been one of the faculty who pushed her down because they were all standing apart from the students. Finally, one of her senior girls came and helped her up and helped her walk to her house which is adjacent to the campus. She tried to go to class then but was hurting too badly. She stayed home for two days and then limped back to class. The following Saturday she said she was getting a little better but then her legs swelled up quite a bit and the pain was worse. She did go to the hospital, which is another story in itself, and what finally happened was the security guard who was helping her find her way around there and some staff member advised her to go to a private doctor in town which they recommended which she ended up doing; I think they even made the appointment for her. He checked her over, gave her some meds for a diuretic, blood thinner, and pain; her bill for the lot was $28 U.S. She was feeling better just in less than a day. He did mention giving her tests but she said if this was necessary she would go to Windhoek, Cape Town or back home to Washington, D.C. and stay there. I certainly understood this. She has traveled a lot, lived in other countries, and taught English mostly at the university level in the foreign countries so she has taken care of herself pretty well and is certainly no “shrinking violet”.

Payday here starts on the 21st of the month with many getting paid on the last few days of the month; I believe the policemen and guards get paid first. There are very long lines at the ATM machines because the pay is deposited in the bank for the workers. I don’t think many of the people had checking accounts, per se. It was cash and carry, so to speak. On Friday afternoons and Saturday mornings especially, it was like a zoo downtown with all the people, cars, taxis, trucks, and the regular shops and open markets having long lines. The bars/*shebeens* were crowded, as well. It seems there is always money for drink when payday comes around. It appeared that many people were almost out of money by the end of the month as is the case in other countries, as well. Of course, all of the standing water and mud added to the confusion. The stores close in the early afternoon on Saturday. On Friday, on my way home from the bank, I decided to stop at the grocery store and take my chances; it wasn’t too bad. You just knew that you had to wait and in the lines if you leave more than 3 inches between you and the person in front of you, someone will try to squeeze in. I took a taxi back because I had too much to carry for the twenty minute walk home. Taxis are N$7.50 for anywhere in town. When we go to the next biggest town about 40 km away it costs N$12 or$13; we think this is pretty good.

More and more rain kept falling so now the lake in front of the school was even bigger. The custodians and the older school boys had been filling sandbags and dragging them to the needed places. There was plenty of sand around. These were really heavy. They weren't small like the ones I saw on TV last year when people were sandbagging in Mt. Vernon, WA, north of where I live in the state, to keep the levee water from going to the downtown area. Some SUV's and 4WDs could go across the water but nothing else; I didn't know how long they would be able to do this. Mr. Caparros next door finally had his car towed out near the street so he could use it since he could not get through the water with it. He paid someone to guard it during the night so no one would steal it. The makeshift walkway from the street to the school was still holding up most of the time. My house was behind the school so this wasn't a problem for me but when I walked downtown I had to wade out through the water. On one particular Friday I could walk on the walkway with regular walking shoes without getting too wet but Saturday I wore my Teva sandals because there was about 2 more inches of water and some of the boards and bricks had sunk down a bit. It was more of a challenge the next morning when school was in session again. My principal said that at night when she heard the rain she got a stomach ache wondering what the situation would be in the morning. A lot of the girls and women were wearing the crocs or some other kind of "jelly" shoes. Well, THIS, TOO, SHALL PASS, I thought, and after the winter months when it is really hot and dry as dust, we might long for the wet times. I didn't know what was coming next for me.

EXPERIENCING NATIONAL HEALTHCARE-NAMIBIA STYLE

Chapter 10--March 2 & 3, 2009

After experiencing National Healthcare, if this is an example of it, I have reservations about it. I do realize this is a third world country and things are probably better in the first and second world countries that have national healthcare, however I do have some friends in England and Canada who do choose to go to a private doctor rather than waiting in the queue to be served. In the case of some Canadians, they opt to come to the States to have medical procedures done in preference to waiting a long time to be put on the schedule. I had a freak accident on a Monday morning, March 2nd. The end result of this was that I had a broken patella in my right knee and was in a plaster of paris cast from mid-thigh to ankle for six weeks and was on crutches.

To go back to the beginning, I was trying to open my front door, which had always been difficult at best, to get back in the house after going to school. I always had to tug and hit it with my hip a few times for it to open. With all the rain that we'd had, it was swollen even more and in my giving it a few extra licks, it opened and I went flying inside and landed on my right knee on the tile floor. The knee did swell up a bit and hurt some but I thought I could "shake it off" and walked back up near the front of the school to see what was going on because the water was even deeper at the entrance and on the makeshift walkway that had been built. The principal and others were outside the gate in front sending the learners home for the day. I was busy taking pictures of the whole watery scene. The Ministry of Education had been called and came to inspect the situation. After driving through the whole area in his 4 WD truck, he deemed that pre-grade through grade 4 should not come to school for two weeks, but grades 5 through 10 would attend Monday through Friday, although no one would attend on this Monday. A number of the older children did stay for the day and helped with some necessary tasks such as reinforcing the temporary walkway, carrying bricks and filling more sandbags. Some of the teachers stayed for the day.

My morning was spent on catching up on my email, marking copy books and making lesson plans. I was feeling pretty good but after I tried to stand up a few hours later, the knee was very painful. Almost at the same time, Mrs. C., my very kind neighbor, came and told me they were going to take me to a doctor. They discussed private doctors and decided which was best but it would cost $150 Nam; I said this was fine with me. I wanted to go to a private doctor rather than the hospital south of Ondangwa. There was the situation of getting out to the main road because of the flooding. We had to wait for the *bakki* 4WD, to come back from hauling bricks up to the walkway to get out to the street. Mr. C. couldn't drive his car, as I mentioned before. Mr. Mwai, who was going to take me, had his car parked up at the entrance since a regular car couldn't get through "Lake Heroes", as I called it. When we finally got up to the road, Mr. M., his wife and Mrs. C. were with me. As he kept driving I just knew we were on the way to the hospital and I wanted to shout, "No, no, I don't want to go there", but since he was kind enough to drive me, I couldn't complain so this is where we went. His wife (who was the pre-grade teacher at Heroes) knew a doctor there whom she liked. Actually two of the teachers at our school had husbands who are doctors there. Both of the families had emigrated from Zimbabwe in the past year to escape the hostilities that were occurring there during the last few years.

There were many many people waiting on benches at the different medical areas. They are so patient and just keep sitting hoping to get a turn to see a medical person. No one has anything to read while waiting as some of us choose to do in this country. First, we stopped at Admitting to get a Medical Passport which Mr. and Mrs. M. negotiated for me. This didn't take very long (by Namibian standards); we were told to go to Casualty. This department is for broken bones and accidents. I was limping quite badly at this point even with hanging onto two people. I think all those people waiting on the benches could see that I was in pain by the way I was walking and groaning occasionally, so maybe they understood about my not waiting in line. The nurse who took all the information was very nice and gave me an injection in the hip for pain which helped greatly and after about ten minutes, I felt no more pain nor the following day; it must have been a mighty dose. She said she would "beg" the doctor to see me. He seemed knowledgeable and after a few questions sent me to x-ray.

The technician said they had just gotten a new machine and it did look pretty good. The result of this showed a broken bone in the patella. I was wheeled back to the doctor whereupon I was told that I would possibly have to have surgery and this would be done at the hospital in Oshakati which was about forty kilometers away. This made my heart skip a beat. I asked him how soon and he replied, "Now, today." It was about 3:00 PM at this point. I wanted to go back to the house to get a few things which presented another problem of securing a vehicle to cross the standing water in front of the school. Mrs. C. and I had talked earlier of taking a taxi to the other hospital and she would stay with one of her relatives while I was in the hospital. Hindsight, you know-it is what we should have done. But someone at the hospital south of Ondangwa had told Mr. M. that they would arrange transportation for me to go there in an ambulance.

Mr. M. brought us back to the school and there was the problem of getting over the water again. The *bakki* had gone home for the day so Mr. C. called someone else to come; this involved about an hour of waiting again. You see all this water really COMPLICATED things because I wasn't able to walk out to the main road even to take a taxi to town but my neighbors and teacher friends offered to do anything for me that I needed to have done and, believe me, <u>I'm forever grateful to them</u>. Mr. C. had called one of our school board members to come to take me back to the house to "gather a few things" for my hospital stay. This man often visited the school and had a delightful daughter in grade seven; she was one of my favorites, although teachers aren't supposed to have favorites. When we were at the house I noticed that he examined the door which was the cause of my misfortune.

Back at the hospital I was told several times that the ambulance was on the way. We had arrived back there about 5:00 PM and I told Mr. and Mrs. M. to go home; I could wait by myself. They had taken their three children back home in the morning and were helping with tasks at school for the rest of the day. They suggested that I get something to eat at the snack bar there because they didn't know if I would get any food at the hospital, so I gave them some money to get it for me; I didn't think I would be able to walk that far. They came back with chips, cookies and some fruit drinks. I checked on the status of the ambulance a few times and was always told that it was on the way and I would just have to wait patiently. Sharon and Angela, colleagues whose husbands were doctors there did come by to see me when they heard what happened. Text messages apparently had been flying through the air. They lived close by. I asked them if they had any influence about getting the ambulance, but they didn't. Meanwhile Evelyn called for a friendly chat to say, "How are things going?" When I told what had happened she was very surprised and concerned because of her recent experience at this same hospital with her "ghost" experience. She asked if I had contacted our field director in Windhoek which I hadn't nor had I even thought of it so, she called her right away. She thought I should contact Dr. Kapia, owner of the school, to tell what had happened and perhaps she could advise me about the ambulance. I did this and was hoping she would offer to drive me to Oshakati but she didn't, however she did want to know when I was actually in the vehicle going north. I had to stand most of the time because there was no bench space available. All the benches were still full of patients waiting patiently (pardon the pun) for their turn. I did have my wheeled backpack with me which acted somewhat like a crutch or cane. I <u>could not</u> get a crutch or a wheelchair. I don't know if the personnel didn't understand me or chose to simply ignore me, probably the latter.

About three hours later an ambulance did come to take me to the Oshakati Hospital. Apparently the hospital contracts drivers when they need them or maybe this is just after hours because at this later time, the doctor came out of his office to tell me that as soon as the driver could get transportation to the hospital, he would be there. I called Dr. Kapia back to tell her the ambulance had arrived and I was on my way. This driver told me that he is contracted to drive all kinds of vehicles from various businesses. He has been trying to get a job with one company but so far it hadn't happened. He also said his wife is a teacher in one of the schools in Ondangwa. By the time I arrived at Oshakati it was about 9:00 PM. He arranged for a wheelchair and I was wheeled into the hospital by an attendant. He took me into one of the examining rooms and put a clean sheet on the bed although I never did get onto the bed. I called my neighbors back in Ondangwa to tell them of my progress because they were very worried about me. Marissa told me to ask for a private room. A few people came by to look at my x-ray and medical passport then left. Finally a doctor did come by to tell me that he was going to admit me. I asked how many people were in the hospital, thinking of what Marissa had said. He related it wasn't very full at this time.

Sometime later I was wheeled down to Ward 6. It seemed like we went for ten minutes turning at one corridor and then another. This is the main hospital in the area and it is all on one floor so the campus is quite large in area. I was not impressed at all once we arrived. The time was 10:00 PM by now. The place looked dirty and the toilets smelled. My heart sank a little and my stomach turned a little but I thought, "I can do this; I can cope." After about five minutes the two nurses at the table there at the entrance looked at me and asked why I was there. I related that I had a fractured patella and possibly needed surgery. I gave one of them my x-ray and medical passport. One said, "Well, we have no room for you here; we can't put you in with anyone who is sick." I must say that I didn't look sick compared to most of the people I saw. I said, "I suppose I can spend the night in my wheelchair." One patient was on a gurney (they call it a *trolley)* under a pile of blankets and another was on the floor on a mat under a blanket. The next morning there were two more people lying in the corridor.

The nurses seemed to take their time about doing any and everything; I noticed this throughout the hospital the next day that many are talking on their cell phones while attending patients or doing nothing else. Yes, the cell phone addiction is alive and well in Namibia, as it is in the States. At any rate, Julia, the nurse, did take me to a four-bed ward where there was an unoccupied bed which did have a clean sheet on it. This was about 11:00 PM; I felt that she had "warmed" up to me a little bit by this time. I asked her if I could use the toilet first, so she wheeled me in there. It really smelled but "when you have to go, you have to go." Then I asked for TP so she brought me a roll and told me to keep it. The door wouldn't close with the wheelchair but I didn't care about this. When we returned to the room, she helped me into bed because it was very high, then I asked, "Shall I just keep my clothes on?" to which she replied in the affirmative. She put my backpack up by my pillow because "it would be safer there," she explained. The lights were on very brightly so I asked if she would turn them off which she did about midnight but then they were turned on about 4:30 AM next morning. She told me the surgeon would see me in the morning. I did sleep for a few hours. I thought, "What am I doing here and what are they going to do to me?" The other three people in the room were quite ill, I could see. There were two women and one man.

I did wheel myself to the toilet once during the night but the next morning my wheelchair was gone and I couldn't walk on my right leg. I hopped over to the sink in the corner of the room to wash my face and brush my teeth. There was some kind of a large dead insect in the basin but I used it anyway. It was too far to hop to the toilet but I did get a bedpan some forty-five minutes later after asking for help. The nurses and/or aides kept walking up and down the corridor but none came to the room and when one finally did, I flagged her down. The ward did look a little better in the daytime than the night before because someone did come in early to sweep, then mop the floor..

Evelyn called about 8:00 AM to see how things were. When I told her I might have to have surgery, she told me to get a second opinion before letting anyone cut on me. She suggested going to a private hospital in Ongwediva, a town between Oshakati and Ondangwa; I had not thought of this. She asked if our field director had called me yet and was quite upset that she hadn't. Jocie did call about 9:00 AM and said that she understood I was having a little medical problem. I replied, "Yes, I fell and broke my patella." She suggested that perhaps I might want to go to the private hospital in Ongwediva and I readily decided to do this. (I did find one sentence later in our thick handbook referring to this hospital.) My problems were that I couldn't walk, the medical staff seemed to be ignoring me, I didn't have the hospital's number and had no transportation. Jocie said she would call Chris, a fellow World Teach colleague who was in a town north of where I was about an hour's drive away, to see if he could assist me. He and his wife, Chloe, were always willing to help in anyway they could. I decided when he arrived I would ask him to take me to the private hospital.

Whenever I asked when the doctor would be there, the answer was always, "He's coming." I explained this expression earlier which can mean in a few minutes, a few hours or days, or even a few weeks. At this point I was hoping the doctor would not come to examine me before Chris arrived because things never seemed to happen quickly in Namibia. As it turned out, Dr. Michael **did** arrive before Chris did along with two nurses pushing the trolley. He said he was from Eastern Europe but we found out later he was from Russia; I don't know why he didn't want to say that. I don't know how he happened to be in Namibia but the majority of doctors seem to be from other countries because Namibia doesn't have a medical school as yet, but the University of Namibia in Windhoek is working on this. The first thing he said to me was that I had a terrible accent for English; I thought, "Yours isn't so hot yourself, Buster," but I didn't say anything since he might be holding the scalpel later on. He made his diagnosis saying surgery wasn't necessary but a cast would take care of the situation; I was relieved to hear this. I told him I wanted to go to a private hospital and a friend was coming to help me so wanted to wait until he arrived before anything was done. Dr. Michael said I could go to London, Paris or New York but the cast would have to be applied.

As it turned out, they got into action (for a change), put me on the trolley and we were headed out of the ward to x-ray, I thought. At this moment Chris called saying he was at the main gate of the hospital and would meet us at x-ray, but we weren't there because I had misunderstood. I had my cell phone with me all the time which was a Godsend and had enough minutes on it for the various calls I had to make. We went to the POP room to have the procedure done; I'm guessing this may have meant Plaster of Paris but I don't know for sure. It took Chris about fifteen minutes to find us. Dr. Michael and the nurses asked me what he looked like and I replied that he was tall, about thirty years old, has red hair and light skin like mine; at that moment he popped in through the doorway.

Dr. Michael was just finishing wrapping the cast. He explained to Chris what he had done and why and showed him the x-ray. He was impressed with the doctor which made me feel a little better. Next we went to x-ray to have another one taken to see if anything had moved but apparently things seemed to be fine. Chris was running back and forth between departments fetching and delivering items on my behalf. He found out, as well, that sometimes when he was told to go to one place, he was sent back to where he started. Apparently the right hand doesn't know what the left is doing and vice versa. I don't know what it is but we think that rather than saying they don't know the answer, they just send a person to another location. I am so grateful that he was there; it would have been a lot more difficult for me had I not had an advocate there. It was lying there not knowing if the hospital staff was doing anything about my situation or just ignoring it, and my not being able to walk or speak the language really complicated things. I told Chris how much I appreciated his coming to my aid and hoped he hadn't missed anything really important at his school that day. He said he had only two math classes that day and a staff meeting that would probably drone on for a few hours which he REALLY hated to miss.

Earlier Dr. Michael said I would have to stay another night and I thought, "Oh, no, not another night in Ward 6." I was wheeled back to the ward to my bed. What I needed was some crutches but the nurse said

I would have to show my passport which I didn't have. I hadn't taken anything of value with me but I did have some NAM money. Chris offered to use his passport but this was not acceptable. Then I said I would pay for the crutches so she told him to go talk to the Casualty office where the crutches were. I gave him $200 to cover whatever he had to pay. He went back there; you must realize that almost every time he had to go to a different place it seemed to be across the campus. When he returned to Casualty he was told he had to go to Administration which he did, but it was closed until 2:00 PM. It was 1:15 at this time so I suggested he might want to go for a walk or get something to eat. He did come back a little before 2 to report that he was off to Administration. When he arrived there he was told he needed to go to Casualty because that department takes care of the crutches so he went back there. There was no one there to help him but he saw the room where the crutches were, found someone my size, the two of them went in the room, tried several crutches and selected two that he thought would be right for me. He did a good job with that because they did fit pretty well. The only problem was that the rubber tips (they call them shoes) were worn through but I was able to get new ones later on back in Ondangwa. At this point I was happy to have anything that looked like a crutch. Chris went back and talked to the doctor, who in the end dismissed me that afternoon. I had told him that I would have someone to take care of me at home. I knew the Caparros' and Evelyn would help out even without asking them ahead of time. Later on, Chris said when he was walking around on my behalf, different hospital personnel asked him how his mother was doing and he replied, "Fine." I was glad they hadn't asked, "How is your grandmother doing?"

This is a note about the food there as I was wondering if any meals were served. I had read that in some countries the families have to bring food to the patients if they want something to eat. In the morning there was a plate on the stand by my bed that had porridge which tasted like grits with a ground beef gravy. There was no utensil with the plate. I hadn't even seen the food there but the lady in the next bed pointed it out when I happened to look at her. I said something like, "No spoon", and she motioned for me to eat it with my fingers. I looked in my backpack and found a little plastic spoon which I used. When I came back after the "cast procedure" there was a plate with rice, a small piece of chicken mostly of skin and bone and pork and beans. I ate some of that; it did taste good but I didn't have much of an appetite throughout all of this.

The final checkout procedure was getting the meds which consisted of some pain pills and multivitamins, of all things. This didn't take very long and then I was to make my final payment of NAM $30 for my fee at the pharmacy. I had already paid $35 NAM for the crutches. We were told the $30 had to be paid at another place so Chris took off again but soon came back saying he was told that it had to be done at the pharmacy so this was done. He found out that since we were volunteers in the country, we were not considered foreigners, so a passport had not been needed for anything.

While I was waiting out in the car for Chris, Dr. Kapia did call and offered to take me back to Ondangwa. She was in her Oshakati optometrist clinic this day. I thanked her but said that other arrangements had been made so I knew she was looking out for me. Meantime I had called Mr. Caparros saying that I was coming home that day; Chris would drive me to Ondangwa where we were going to pick up Evelyn who would stay with me for the night. I asked if he could arrange for a vehicle to get me over the water out in the front of the school. They had planned to come to the private hospital to see me the next afternoon but I informed him that plans had changed. He did arrange this and the vehicle was there in front of the school when we arrived so I was home instead of still at the hospital in Ward 6. My entire expenses for the two hospitals was N$78 which equates to about $8 U.S. but I would have been willing to pay more to have gone to a private hospital. After this experience I was going to try very hard to avoid any more medical facilities. When I went in the front door, I noticed the door had been planed or sanded down so it would open more easily. I suppose I should have said something before, but I just thought, "this is the way things are in Namibia." I know it takes a long time or maybe never to get things fixed. The next day Mrs. Gulu, my principal, told me that since this was a private school, we didn't have to wait for the government to repair things.

Dr. Michael told me to get a lot of rest for one week and not be up and about except when it was really necessary. I wasn't in any pain but I felt very tired. I didn't know how long it would be before I could go back to teaching my classes. He suggested in jest, I think, that I go to London or Paris for a month to recuperate which was really a laugh since I couldn't even get out to the Main Road, besides, who was going to pay for this? Evelyn spent the night with me which helped a lot and she said she would come back whenever I asked. She was getting better from her "ghost incident" but her legs were swollen. She is tall and slim and her legs would look good on anyone but for her this wasn't normal. Her boarding school was closed for the week because the rain and sewage were getting mixed up so all the learners were sent home. Mrs. C. and Marissa fixed enough dinner for about three days and it was still warm when they brought it over.

Now it was on to the recovery stage. I thought I might be able to go back to teaching the next week but there was the problem of the water and the makeshift walkways. Mrs. Gulu told me the next morning that they were trying to arrange for someone to take over my classes until I returned but this didn't happen so my learners had a free period when I was supposed to be there. The other teachers had more classes than I did and all of our times tables were different; I thought I might be able to go back in two weeks. Actually I only missed eight days because that first Monday school was closed and on Friday of the second week there was a district teacher's meeting so there were no classes that day.

ARE YOU FEELING A LITTLE FINER, MISS NORENE?

Chapter 11--The Recovery-March and April, 2009

My BIG NEWS at this time was that I had a brand new pair of crutches that fit me better and had very substantial rubber "shoes" because a Physical Therapist came by to bring them to me. One of the staff suggested I call him about getting rubber tips that weren't worn through. She gave me his name and phone number. When I first talked to him on the phone he told me to bring the crutches down to his office and he would see what he could do. I explained that there was no way I could get out of here to see him, so he called me that night and said he would come to see me. It turned out that he is familiar with the school having once been on the Board of Trustees, having children who attended here, knows some of the staff, and knows my next-door neighbors really well, the ones who have been so kind to me, so-o-o I guess we were all one big happy family. He is from Tanzania, was very friendly and I did like him. On that first visit he adjusted those first crutches somewhat and said he would be back. The next week he came with new crutches and told me to call him any time if I need anything. He said when he first saw me that since I had no pain, this meant things were healing properly.

Most of my colleagues encouraged me to take more time off but I was ready to do something useful. I felt like I was on a first name basis with the several spiders that lived on the walls and ceiling of my kitchen/living room combo. They didn't really bother me and I think they are helpful, however I must confess that I did kill a few at times. I didn't mind six or eight but when they had babies, this was a little too many for a house of this size, I felt. I was caught up on my e-mail, had made future lesson plans, read the one book that I had, so was getting a little bored. Evelyn and Vic, who were both off from teaching because of the flooding, stopped by one afternoon and tried to encourage me to go on a trip with them for a few days to a cheetah farm and other points of interest in the area, but I declined because I just didn't feel up to it and didn't want to encumber them because of my situation.

I went back to teaching after two weeks and it worked out pretty well. There were two 8th grade girls who came to the house to escort me there and back and helped me get up the two steps that lead into each classroom. I believe Mr. C. arranged this because I had told him a few days earlier that I thought I could go back to school if I had some help to get up and down the steps and to carry my things. Then on Monday morning these two knocked on my door and said they were there to help me. During the next few weeks I came home after my last class rather than stay there until 3:30 PM. I brought my work home to do where I could sit on the futon with my "casted" leg up off the floor. The leg and foot did swell during the day but it went down at night.

There was another short week because on Monday, there was another teachers' meeting in the circuit somewhere (yippee, I missed it) and Saturday, March 21 was Independence Day so Friday was a holiday. Namibia became independent on March 21, 1989. There were no celebrations in this area that I was aware of, but in the larger towns and cities there were parades and a little more fanfare. Speaking of fanfare, I must tell you about how the President travels. We saw this once when we were coming back from the weekend at Etosha National Park. He has a motorcade which looked to be about as big as the U.S. President's. It takes up both sides of the highway and every motorist has to pull off to the side until the entourage passes. The main highway north from Windhoek is four lanes wide in some places and two lanes in others. The sirens are going and flags are fluttering on the vehicles. Evelyn was uptown last week when the procession came through to inspect the flood situation and was told by one of the pedestrians that she should stop walking until the motorcade passed. In the newspaper The Namibian, there was an article about the President's request for a N$300 million--US $30 mil. which was hidden in the budget for this year. Of course, he denied it but the finance people say it is there in the figures.

Politics seemed to be "alive and well" here in this country as it is in many others.

The water had gone down quite a bit in some places and not a lot in others, but I still was not able to get out until the "lake" in front of the school was gone. It hadn't rained here for about two weeks so I thought maybe the wet season was nearly over. Mr. Caparros still had his car parked out inside the front gate. They had to walk out on the makeshift walkway to get there but at least, they could get out to use it. They have friends and relatives living in Oshakati whom they went to visit almost every weekend.

A few people from the States had written suggesting that I come home and a few strongly **urged** that I get the first plane out of here after my cast was off, but I didn't plan to do this, at least not at that point anyway. I was confident that I would be able to get back to a somewhat normal routine with the physical therapy that I would get when the cast came off. One person even offered to pay, if I would have to pay to get my return ticket changed. I did appreciate everyone's support. I thought my family might say, in light of the mugging and now the broken patella, "Mom, it's time for you to come home," but they didn't. I did talk to them on the phone every few weeks. Phone calls between the two countries were very expensive. My daughter-in-law did set me up with Skype before I went to Namibia, but it was illegal to use it there; also, international phone cards did not work there.

My friend, Evelyn, had been coming over about twice a week to visit and fix dinner for the two of us. I really appreciated her support, as well as everyone else's. I was blessed to have such good friends to help take care of me. I told her that after the cast was off I would take her out to dinner and the sky was the limit. I said that I felt guilty because I didn't go over to help her when she was knocked down during the "ghost" incident at her school, although we had met uptown for lunch on Saturdays. A few people wrote about incidents happening in "threes" about which she and I had talked. First it was the mugging on January 16, then her ghost incident and now my patella situation. We didn't even want to think about Number 3.

As I mentioned above, my family had called a few times recently; I did miss them and friends, but I never felt homesick or morose. With my schoolwork and my internet I was busy most of the time. I thought when I was able to be out and about again I would buy a radio, perhaps shortwave, so I could get some news; I didn't miss the TV because I don't watch it very much when I am home. I looked up the New York Times, Reuters, and The Seattle Times on the internet sometimes to see what was going on and, of course, I received the news from family and friends, as well, which was mostly about the economy which was not getting any better. I knew that the snow kept coming in the Puget Sound area: I think it had been a different kind of winter for everyone in the States. In Namibia, we were going into fall but the weather didn't change much. It seemed to be either wet and warm or dry and hot. The teachers had told me that it does get cold in winter so I would soon see what "cold" was there. It was really very pleasant in the morning for a few hours but then it gets really hot around noon and remains this way even into the evening. I slept with the fan on for at least half of the night; I didn't need any top sheet.

When one of my 5th graders came to see me one day when I was still "homebound" she asked, "Are you feeling a little finer, Miss Norene?" I thought this was a different way to put it. I said, "Yes, I am a lot finer." I did feel good because I had no pain but I did tire more easily; I suppose this was to be expected. My house was right behind the school so a number of the 5th and 7th graders (whom I taught) came to see me when I was off from teaching those two weeks, and later when I was working at home, when they were on break time. My living room windows faced out to the direction where they were playing or going to the water tap to get a drink, so they would come over and talk through the screens.

On April 1, there was "Fun Day" at school and everyone had a great time. It was well organized with many activities. Since I hadn't gone to any staff meetings and had been at school only about half of the time, I wasn't in on any of the planning. I surely hated that---NOT! I didn't go to the staff meetings because a 3 layer brick barricade had been built at the bottom of the door jamb to keep the water from going into the library and this was something I couldn't manage to get across. The whole day was well planned and directed. The learners practiced for Fun Day for the two weeks before, so classes might as well have been suspended for that time with all the learning that was probably not happening. I heard the practice for the cheering contest from my living room when I was there marking my copy books and making lesson plans. Marissa taught them how to do it and then a leader was chosen from that grade to take over. Besides this activity there were sack races, games of different kinds, skits of different types in which the girls seemed to like to dress up as pregnant ladies, choosing a king and queen from grades seven through nine, soccer (football) matches between grades and between boys and girls, singing, dancing, egg attack, water balloons, and the school choir. Grade ten sold drinks, snacks and ice cream cones. There were a few rain showers that day but it didn't dampen anyone's spirits and enthusiasm.

During the Easter holiday, which was Friday, April 10 through Monday April 13, my wonderful neighbors invited me to go with them to Ongwediva and Oshakati to visit their friends and relatives. I was very happy they included me. I was going to get my cast off the next week so I was feeling fine and could walk pretty well despite my encumbrances. They are Filipino, as I mentioned before, and there seems to be a very "tight" Filipino conclave there. I went shopping with them a little bit and was able to handle that but when we were in a home, I just sat around mostly reading the newspaper and the "You" magazines that were there. "You" is published in South Africa and is something like "People" magazine here in the States. The TV was almost always on rather loudly with no one watching it, but me and I only watched because it was there. I did turn it off sometimes but when someone else came in the room, on it went.

The ladies were in the kitchen most of the time fixing food, talking and laughing; I went out to talk and offer my services but they wouldn't let me. Of course, I couldn't speak their language but they did speak English quite well and would use that when talking to me. The men were playing Scrabble in the other room. They did invite me to play and I played two games but I was no match for them. They were really "fierce" players and had the Scrabble dictionary right there. They know all the two and three letter words and their meanings to make lots of points, most of which I never heard of, for instance ee, eu, wa, zo, sao, etc. I do know the game but not the way they knew it. When I questioned them, they said, "Look it up in the dictionary." I did catch them on a few of their words. This one man told me I needed to make words that made more points and would block the opponent who goes next. I knew this but I was just happy to make any word to get my turn over with. Anyway, it was a diversion but I did get tired sitting there on the hard chair that long with my leg with the cast stretched out, so I declined after that.

Their food is pretty highly spiced and some of the dishes had organ meats in them, which I don't care for very much, but I always took some of most of the dishes. There was always steamed rice which I like. I went to Easter mass with them which I enjoyed. I liked the music and singing. There were many people there but we did manage to get chairs in the back of this very large room. I think there were three white people there: the priest, another man and myself. The man, South African, is married to a relative of the Caparros. We went to their home after the service for a snack and then went back to the house and had lunch about an hour later. It seemed like we were always eating or getting ready to eat. Everyone was always very kind to me and asked if I was feeling well. Evelyn had gone to Windhoek for the long weekend to see a few points of interest but reported, when she returned, that most things were closed because of the Easter holiday, but she did relax and read.

The BIG DAY for me to get the cast off was April 14 when I went to see Dr. Bandiaihi, the physical therapist. I left right after school was out; Rina drove me there; she borrowed Mr. C.'s car because I didn't think I was quite ready to go out to Main Road and flag down a taxi. I didn't have to wait more than a few minutes to see him. He wasn't quite sure about removing the cast, so told me I might need to go back to the Oshakati Hospital. He sent me to have another x-ray taken and the technician remembered me from six weeks before. He probably doesn't have many white patients with red hair. He was very friendly again. After looking at the x-ray Dr. B showed me where the bone was growing together but said a screw might have to be put in and I thought, "Oh, no, don't tell me that." I wanted to put my head down and cry but I didn't. So he didn't remove the cast but assured me that it would be removed at the other hospital the next day, for sure. He called a doctor there, whom he knew, to say that I was coming in the morning. They don't exactly make appointments but things go a little faster if someone intercedes on the patient's behalf. I thought if a screw had to be put in, I was going to the private hospital for sure.

I decided to take the next day off and go up there in the morning because you can't believe the number of people who are there from noon on sitting patiently in the queue on the benches without backs. I had only one class in the morning and thought I would be back to school by the afternoon. The next morning I told the principal that I wanted to take the day off, or however long it took, to go to the hospital and asked if she could arrange transportation for me. I was thinking of taking a taxi but it would have to come in from the street over the sandbag driveway because I couldn't walk out there. She and some others standing there didn't want me to take a taxi because "I might not be able to trust them" they said, so she asked one of the teachers to drive me there, and stay until I was finished, which he did. She was always very accommodating with me and others.

We arrived at the hospital about 9:00 AM and Mr. Elago went in to find out where I was supposed to go-Room 23-and waited with me until we were sure that I would be taken care of, then I told him he didn't have to stay right with me because after the consultation I would go to the

POP room to have the cast removed, then to x-ray, next back to room 23 again then I would call him when I was finished. I had to wait about 30 minutes to see Dr. Ruusa, a rather sturdy female doctor from Russia, whom Dr. B. had talked to the day before. She was efficient and friendly. I have no complaint about the doctors who dealt with me during this situation; they all seemed to know what they were doing. At the POP room, which is in one part of Casualty, I waited forty-five minutes. One patient was in there all that time; I could hear the saw going part of the time. Finally I went over to one of the orderlies to ask when my turn was and I did get in soon after that. The technician was not friendly at all; I tried to make a little pleasant conversation but he wasn't interested and since he had the saw in his hand I didn't pursue it any further. Since I had never seen this procedure before, I didn't know what to expect. It was a small circular saw which he guided right down the top center of the cast. I felt a little heat and thought I hope he doesn't have to cough or sneeze. Then he had some really long pliers that he opened the cut in the plaster with and pried it off, and then it was over. He said, "Finished, get off the table" so I hopped down.

Believe me, I was so **happy** to have it off. The technician told me to use the crutches to go to x-ray and I did need them for security. I thought I would be able to throw away the crutches right away but this was not the case. I was surprised at how much muscle tone and strength I had lost in the six weeks. My knee was stiff but nothing hurt and I was walking better each day. I knew it would take time to get back to somewhat normal. I saw Dr. Michael (the surgeon who put the cast on) when I got back to Room 23; he checked me over and out and said I didn't have to go back to him. I was told to use one crutch when I'm outside but could walk inside with no props. I had a telescopic hiking stick that I brought with me and this is what I used rather than the crutch; it looks like a cane and worked very well. The Oshakati Hospital looks pretty good up front and it is clean in the rooms where patients are seen; the x-ray room is pretty modern but back in the wards is what turned me off. At least I didn't have to go back in one of those smelly buildings this time. When I arrived back at school and walked across to the staff room, many of the 5th graders were outside there and came running over to greet me shouting, "Here's Miss Norene without the cast." They seemed happy to see me and this made me feel really good! So-o-o ends the tale of the cast but I did go back to Dr. B. twice for exercises to do and for him to have a look at me.

During the last two weeks of April, everyone was engrossed in the term ending exams. I've mentioned before that the Ministry of Education is really big on testing and the teachers and learners take it very seriously.

On my first "castless" weekend, Evelyn and I went to Oshakati on Saturday to shop, get a haircut, have carrot cake and good coffee, stay in a nice hotel on Saturday night and return on Sunday. I bought a radio/CD/ cassette player. There were several World Teach volunteers there doing their weekly shopping, since it is the only large town in the area and it was fun seeing them and exchanging experiences. We all ate at the KFC restaurant there since it was the closest eating place to the largest shopping mall in town. They were all happy to see me without the cast and being able to walk almost normally. Of course, I was the happiest of all. Steve, one of the volunteers who has his own car, drove Evelyn and me to the hotel so we didn't have to go by taxi, and then we talked to him for an hour or so while having a drink. He was in his second year of teaching in Namibia. I had not talked to him very much before so it was interesting to get to know him a little better. We had a nice room, a good dinner, a warm shower, and then a very ample breakfast; these were some of the pleasures in our lives at this point.

Now my thoughts were about my upcoming trip to Zambia, Botswana, and then back to Windhoek, which I made plans for in February over the internet. There were no travel agents in the northern part of the country, so thank goodness for the internet. There was a break from April 26 to May 26 from school between Terms 1 and 2. I had already paid for most of this so I was determined to get well enough to do it. This gave me an added incentive.

The rains had stopped, a lot of the water had evaporated, the bricks had all been picked up by the learners and some of the sandbags were now being used as a driveway across the remaining water in front of the school--rather bumpy--like some of the roads around here, but it worked and all vehicles could travel over it. So life went on in the village of Ondangwa; I was looking forward to my holiday and I really felt BLESSED!

AN UNFORGETTABLE HOLIDAY

Chapter 12--Zambia, Botswana, Windhoek-May 2009

How refreshing it was to have a holiday from school to explore more of Africa! One of my long desires was to be accomplished now, this being seeing the amazing Victoria Falls. This started on April 29; the first step to getting there was to take a "Combi" bus from Ondangwa to a town south of here (about a 2 ½ hour drive) to catch the Capeliner which goes from Cape Town, South Africa to Livingstone on the Zambia side of Victoria Falls. It goes from Cape Town east to Johannesburg, as well, and to some other points plus being relatively on time and much cheaper than flying and one's reservation is assured on it.

This was my first experience with the Combi. These are passenger vans and small buses that have a definite destination on which you can make a reservation the day before, but they will not leave until they are full of passengers or nearly full. I have a friend who stayed the night with me the Friday before I left, who took the same Combi from here to Tsumeb which was my destination. She was up even before I awoke, arrived at the departing place at 6:00 AM, but the van did not leave until 2:00 PM. I was luckier because I was there at 7:15 AM and we left at 9:45 AM. I took a book to read while sitting on the bus waiting for it to get full. There are always a number of buses lined up with many young men trying to get any person arriving to get on "their" bus. They are like a bunch of locusts plus they are so tall and I'm so short; I just smiled and kept saying, "No, thank you" although I want to scream and say, **"Please leave me alone."**

I had made a reservation in the town of Tsumeb, where I would board the Capeliner, at a B & B relatively close to the departing place because of the uncertainty of the Combi, so I had a restful day and a half there. It is a very beautiful town unlike Ondangwa. The motel provides security for its guests going on the bus because it arrives about midnight and it is just unsafe any place here in Africa to be out walking after dark even though the B & B was only a few blocks from where the bus would arrive. This was assuring to me.

Quite by accident I sat by a young man on the bus who was a brother of one of my colleagues who was teaching northeast of Ondangwa. He had been traveling two days from Australia to meet his brother, James, and they were going to Victoria Falls and some other places. We picked up James about 6:00 AM the next morning. It was good to see him, as well; he was leaving the World Teach program soon because he had been granted a fellowship for five years at MIT in Massachusetts and he well deserved this. After this I sat with a young Zambian man, Mike, who was a volunteer working with a group of very underprivileged people teaching mainly Life Skills to adults and basic education to the children in the Cape Town area. He was going back to Zambia on a "working holiday" for two months in a church program to help teens and young adults with strategies to have a better life. It was stressed many times over to get a better education to get ahead because unemployment is at a high level in many African countries–over 20 to 30 %-from what I heard and read, so it is difficult to get a job without an advanced education or a needed skill, just as it is in other countries.

Zambia

The town of Victoria Falls in Zimbabwe was the preferred place to go, it seems, until all the trouble erupted in Zimbabwe a few years ago, so now the town of Livingstone has more of the tourist trade. When we crossed the border between Namibia and Zambia, all non-Zambians had to pay $50 U.S. for a visa to enter the country. Many of the people on the bus departed before we came to the border. Upon arriving in Livingstone, we had to go through the mad scramble of young men trying to get you in "their" taxi. Mike helped me get to a taxi which overcharged me because I didn't have any kwasha, the Zambian money. They didn't want Namibian money and I wasn't about to give them U.S. dollars so I paid what they asked. I found on this trip that no one wants Namibian money and you can't exchange it even at the banks for the local money. The kwasha money is into the hundreds of thousands but it is stable now. A nice meal costs 80,000 to 100,000 K which is probably about $14 or $15 U.S. I asked someone why they don't just knock off 3 zeroes but they aren't ready to do this yet, I suppose it would cost a lot of money to print new money and change the banking system, etc. In Zimbabwe their money was up into the millions and billions so they have suspended that and are using South African rand and U.S. dollars. I was surprised and somewhat pleased to see that the American dollar seems to be popular in some of those countries.

My accommodations were at the rustic Maramba River Lodge on the Zambezi River in a safari tent (permanent) with shared ablutions. My friend Beverly, whom I would see in Lusaka, suggested this lodge as a favorite of theirs and it turned out to be a wonderful and affordable place to stay. I really enjoyed my tent, when in the evening and early night I listened to the frogs' sounds which sounded like musical wind chimes. Breakfast and dinner were served out on the patio part of the dining room overlooking the river. There was a family of hippos that seemed to live there but I saw them only once.

The receptionist Bridget arranged several safaris for me in which she had to make a number of phone calls. This was done mostly on Saturday afternoon after I arrived because I wanted to get those things taken care of as soon as possible. Then she had to check the day before for each one to see if there were enough bookings for the activity to proceed. On the second day I said, "I think maybe I ask too many questions," to which she replied, "I've grown to understand you."

On Sunday morning, I took a helicopter ride to view Victoria Falls; there were five of us in the copter plus the pilot. I was able to sit up by the pilot so had a really good view; it is an amazing sight. The Falls was really full because of all the rain that had fallen in the summer. It is just very difficult to describe this natural wonder. The weather was sunny with very few clouds in the sky which added more beauty to this sight. I don't know if there are any view points on the ground where one can see the whole falls at once from the Zambia side. In the afternoon I took a taxi out there and spent a few hours mostly just looking at the Falls from a few view points.**I might interject here that taxis were about the only mode of transport unless people had their own cars. Everyone is warned about not walking out in the rural areas because of possible muggers. John, the taxi driver that I had several times, took me out and then came back two hours later. On the path on the way to the main viewing area is a bronze statue of Dr. David Livingstone. At the viewing area are raincoats, sandals, umbrellas, etc. for people to rent who want to walk down to the bottom to see the Falls. In another time I would have gone down but after I went a short way and saw how steep and slippery it was, I thought this would not be one of the "smarter things I ever did" considering I was almost recovered from the broken patella. Those who did go down without any raingear came up just drenched but were exhilarated and overjoyed that they had accomplished the feat.

One "challenge" that I had on Sunday morning after the heli ride was when the driver took me back to town so that I could get some kwacha. After two tries the ATM machine took my card. There was a worker in the bank, Charity, who unlocked the door and after listening to my plight, told me to come back on Monday morning and it would all be straightened out. I did this the next morning; there is a lot of waiting involved in everything that one does and you need to show your passport to each new person who helps you. First, I had to wait for someone to give me my card; it was locked in his desk. Then I asked him to go out with me while I tried the machine; it still wouldn't work so he concluded it was the machine at fault. The next wait was for someone to come who could fix the machine. Finally it did get all straightened out and after this I had no trouble using any ATM. One U.S. dollar equals 5500 to 6000 kwacha and about $7.50 Namibian. I think I had it all sorted out by the time I left the country. The kwacha is all bills: 500; 1000; 5000; 10,000; and 50,000. Maybe there are higher ones but I didn't see any, if there are. The banks and some of the businesses won't accept any U.S. dollar bills unless they are nearly new. If they are wrinkled, have fold marks, folded corners, or any tears, they won't take them, even though some of their money is really "ratty" looking. I found this out when I paid for one of the safaris with $60 U.S. The agent called and then came back to the lodge later to return my money and collect 330,000 kwacha from me. Fortunately I had that. When I withdrew $200 U.S., I had to key in 1,200,000 to get that amount in kwacha. Enough about money!!

When I was walking along the street after the ATM solution, I saw Mike, my seatmate on the Capeliner, and greeted him like a long lost friend. We talked a bit; he said he had been thinking about me and wondered if I was alright. He got one of his "taxi" friends to take me back to the lodge for half the price that I had paid before.

Safaris out of Livingstone

In the afternoon I went on the elephant ride safari with a group to see animals in Mosi-oa-Tunya National Park. We didn't see many animals but it was a pleasant afternoon. At the end of the walk we were able to sit on the knee of "our animal"; mine was Danny and feed them. I enjoyed this very much. I fell in love with Big Danny and treasure that experience. I was the smallest in the group but had the biggest animal. I rode side-saddle because of the recent knee situation. Of all the safaris I was on, most of the other participants were from the expensive hotels: The Royal Livingstone, The Falls, and The Zambezi Sun which go from about $275 to $600+ a night whereas, I was in a safari tent at $55 a night. I did put on my one "dress-up" outfit and go to the Royal Livingstone one night for a "sundowner" dinner overlooking the water. I felt rather elegant and it didn't cost as much as I thought it would Whenever we were getting acquainted, I would tell them that I'm from the Seattle area in the U.S. but am living in Namibia this year and working as a volunteer teacher. Most of them told me what a "noble" thing I'm doing and thanked me for it. I replied that I don't feel noble about anything but am enjoying the experience and trying to do the best I can.

My next venture was on a river safari on the Zambezi on a small boat. There was a young couple from England as well; they were staying at The Falls. I thought they were honeymooners but they said they had been married for several years and this holiday was one of the adventures they wanted to do before the age of 30. This was a great experience because we could get really close to the shore and at one time did go ashore for "morning tea time" and use the "African bathroom" if there was a need, as in "pick any tree or bush that you desire". We saw a number of hippos, one completely out of the water, hammerhead birds, impala, fresh water crocodiles, malachite kingfish, plove, Egyptian geese, and bushbok. There were other birds whose names I can't remember.

Upon arriving back at the lodge I was informed that the walking safari in Mosi-oa-Tunya had been changed from the next morning to this afternoon. This suited me better because I wouldn't have to be ready to go at 6:45 AM; I had chosen the morning because it is cooler then, but the afternoon worked out well. There were five of us on this trip: a younger Canadian couple from Toronto (who were Chinese, I think), our guide, the armed guard, and me. I felt really good walking most of the time (I was using my cane hiking pole) but was getting a bit tired after about 1 and ½ hours but then we stopped to have lemonade and cakes, which was refreshing. We walked somewhat slowly and quietly with the armed guard leading the way ahead of the guide, getting as close to the animals as was safe. On this hike we saw impala, zebra, giraffes, Cape buffalo, baboons, warthogs, crocodiles, snakebirds, and other birds. This was another enjoyable afternoon. When I returned to the lodge I cancelled the game drive that I had booked in that park for the next day because we had been closer to the game than the vehicle would be. So the next day I was free to get ready to go to Lusaka.

I met my "neighbor tenter" that afternoon; no one had been there before. He had been driving from Tanzania and was on the way to South Africa. He had the safari camping vehicle that we see in movies and on TV programs equipped with everything except the tent on top which I did see on a vehicle later. His wife and daughter were with him but his mother-in-law was staying in a hotel. He works at a park in Tanzania but his wife and daughter live in South Africa and they are able to spend three or four months together during the year. He said he felt very fortunate to have a job and be in the situation they are in.

Next morning I went back to Livingstone (the Maramba was 10–12 kilometers from downtown) to buy my ticket for the bus to Lusaka for 80,000 K; this was the business class fare. Then I withdrew 1,000,000 K from the ATM. When I withdrew money in Namibia, the receipt said I had some hundred thousand dollars in my checking account, but in Zambia money I had millions. I should be so lucky!

A Visit to Lusaka-Spending time with Beverly and Philippe

It was an early rise on Thursday morning to be ready for the seven hour trip to Lusaka. John, the taxi driver, came for me and saw me onto the bus and put my bag on. I was able to leave some things at the lodge until my return back there on Monday. The bus was comfortable; my seatmate was an artist from Livingstone who was taking some of his work up to Lusaka to sell. He and his wife are both painters and have had a studio in Livingstone for three years making a living because of the tourist trade. They were teachers before this.

The countryside was green all the way with *bushveld*, some forests, and then flat farming land. The animals grazing in the fields and at the side of the road were cattle and goats. The people do eat pork and lamb but I had not seen any pigs or sheep yet. The *kraals* (the native African huts) are square, whereas in Namibia they are mostly round. Some square concrete block homes have thatched roofs but many are made of corrugated metal. The villages we passed through were very busy. A number of homes had what looked like maize drying on the flat or slightly steeped rooftops. Whenever the bus stopped, people surrounded it selling these products including oranges, bananas, apples, sugar cane, nuts, boiled eggs, drinks, fried fish, chicken and other meats, handcrafts and probably other products that I haven't mentioned.

In the large village of Chowa we stopped for twenty minutes to use the restroom and get something to eat. My artist friend always told me what we were going to do which was helpful. After I got my bag of fried chicken, chips and a bottle of water, I went out to the bus which was already moving. One of the attendants was on the outside and helped me on. I saw that everyone else was on, the door was closed and we were out on the highway. That was a "close call". On the way back I had already decided that I didn't need any more greasy food. I had offered some it to my seatmate but he had brought his lunch. He said it was better for him and I would agree with that.

When I went to get my camera to take some pictures from my shoulder and then my carry-on bag, I found that I didn't have it. I did feel a bit of panic even though it is just a "thing" but later found that after e-mailing the Maramba Lodge, they had found it in the tent where I stayed and were keeping it in the safe until I returned. I was relieved but was sorry that I didn't have it for the Lusaka weekend.

When we arrived at the bus station in Lusaka, my artist "friend" said he would see me to a reliable taxi and see that I got a reasonable fare. As it happened, he saw someone he knew and put me with him. The artist's brother–in-law was meeting him. I never did know his name. I felt safe because he was a large man, Zambian, of course spoke the language, and fended off the young men who descend on anyone looking for a taxi or a bus.

Beverly had e-mailed me the directions to the International School where she teaches and this helped immensely. Here is a bit about Beverly. I met her the summer before in the Seattle area when she came to visit her father during her winter (U.S. summer) break from school. He and his "lady" are in the same dance "group" that my friend, Ron, and I are in. Beverly came to a few of the dances with them; we started talking about Africa since she lived In Zambia and I knew at that time that I was coming to Namibia. She invited me to come to see them if I had a chance and gave me her card with all the information, so this is how it happened. She teaches music at the school--violin (her instrument), piano, theory, appreciation, plus directing the orchestra and choir. Her partner, Philippe, works at the Alliance Françoise in Lusaka. He is French, understands a lot of English, but speaks very little of it. She is fluent in French having lived there while teaching at an International School. She has been with the International Schools in England, France, Germany and now in Zambia for the last two years and just signed a contract for two more years because she likes the school and they like their life there.

They accepted me into their home graciously and showed me every kindness. I felt like their "mama" or "auntie" after a short time. The area where they live reminds me a lot of California where we lived in the Bay Area for so many years with the flowers, fruit, trees, shrubs and climate. She said it is never too hot or too cold.

The next morning we went for a drive to show me the area, then had tea and coffee at a lovely nursery/park area. While she was giving a piano lesson in the afternoon I sat out on the patio in the sun writing postcards. Later in the afternoon it clouded up and began raining really hard, like they and we in Namibia had in January and February, with thunder and lightning, and then hailstones which were up to ½ inch in diameter. Hail is totally unheard of in Zambia. This lasted for about thirty minutes. The trees and plants in their garden really took a beating. Their neighbor next-door said he had never seen this in the thirty years he had lived there.

That evening we went to the opening of the European Film Festival in Lusaka. The embassies had given the faculty tickets for this. Beverly had e-mailed about this before I left Ondangwa, in case I would want to bring one outfit that is a bit dressy. I was looking forward to this since I've never been to a Film Festival even though there is one in Seattle every year. The event was held at the Alliance Françoise, so Philippe knew a number of people there. There was wine and other drinks before the movie started. The first film was Zambian and even though it was in English, I hadn't a clue about what was happening; fortunately it was short. The main feature was Swedish because the president of the Festival that year was from Sweden; it was called "Four Weeks in June" and did have English sub-titles; in a few places the actors did converse in English. We thought it was well done; it was rather dark but ended happily. After the film there were more drinks and hors-d'oeuvres.

The next day Philippe said the battery wasn't charging properly so after he drove it to the shop where they had bought it, it stayed there and couldn't be repaired until Monday; after this we took taxis. I was walking much better by this time and decided I didn't need the cane anymore. They had to get their weekly groceries and after going back to the house, they had planned to have lunch downtown but decided on the Polo Club restaurant which is a short distance from their home. Polo doesn't start until sometime in September, I believe. It was about a ten-minute walk because we weren't allowed to walk across the field but had to go around it. We did see the ponies and then had lunch on the patio overlooking this huge expanse of green lawn. Having never seen a polo field, I didn't realize how very large one is but I suppose there has to be enough room for all ponies to run.

Later in the afternoon Beverly gave me a tour of the school. There are 1200 students enrolled from grades one through twelve. Class size ranges from five to about twenty-three depending upon the subject and there are a very wide range of subjects in the upper levels. Tuition ranges from $8,000 to $28,000 per year. Children of staff members only have to pay 5% of the fee. All of this interested me since I was in education for so many years and was in it now for one more year. It is a bit difficult to get a position in the International Schools program, but once you are in, there are opportunities to move around to different countries within the system, although even this is becoming more difficult now because of the economy.

On Sunday afternoon we took a taxi down to the bus station for me to buy my ticket back to Livingstone. There were only two buses in the morning, 7:00 AM and 10:00 AM so I opted for the 7:00 AM one although it meant a very early rise. Beverly's school starts at 7:00 AM so she didn't have to get up too much earlier to walk me out to the street to get the 6:00 AM taxi to the station. She made arrangements for this with the taxi driver we were using at the time. After this they took me to an open market at one of the shopping centers that has this every Sunday afternoon in the parking lots. It did appear to have "quality" items. Fortunately for me, I did not have space in my bag to take anything extra back. Beverly bought Philippe a medium-sized hippo with a wide-open mouth for his birthday coming up. She wanted to get something he would like and they did look at several different carved wooden objects of art. I bought 2 guinea fowl placemats for her because she said this was her favorite animal. I wanted six but the lady only had two. I did enjoy the afternoon; it is interesting to peruse these open markets.

That night Philippe made his delicious lentil, vegetable, and meat dish for dinner. He was concerned that it was too spicy for me, since I don't like "hot" food, but it was just right. A little more would have been too much. They both like to cook and have their favorites. That afternoon Beverly offered me her phone card to call my children since it was Mother's Day; she said the calls cost very little; I don't know how much "very little" is. Brad had mentioned calling me but my cell phone nor my flexi-call card worked out of Namibia. This may be one more of their exclusionary rules. At any rate, I did talk to my children. I had forgotten about Mother's Day until the day before when I saw merchandise in the store windows advertising the perfect gift for Mother. One was a set of very brief lingerie saying, "This is the perfect gift for Mother on her day." I thought, "Yes, I want that for my Mother's Day gift."

Monday morning came early; I said good-bye to Philippe at the house and then Beverly and I walked out to the front of the school where the taxi was already waiting at 6:00 AM. We said our good-byes; I was really sad to leave them because I had such a wonderful time and they treated me so graciously. I hope they will come to Washington sometime so I can repay them in kind.

The Bus Ride Back to Livingstone

The taxi driver led me through all the hawkers to the correct bus; there were so many of them there even at 6:15 in the morning. It really helps to have someone with you who knows the system. It was a madhouse with dozens of buses and taxis and swarms of people. I found that even though I had paid for business class, I was on the "economy" bus but it all worked out alright. I saw how the "other half" lives and rides. The Africans carry many things in all kinds of suitcases, bags, bundles, and parcels stuffed to the hilt. Most bring food with them for the trip. Hawkers come on the bus to sell cookies, drinks, sweets and jewelry among other things. On business class, sodas and muffins were given to the passengers. Women carry all kinds of goods on their heads plus sometimes a baby on their back and a bag in each hand. Since winter was approaching some people had on heavier sweaters, jackets and hats. I had not felt the need for this yet although some of the children at school had worn fleece tops a lot of the time even when it is hot. I don't see how they stood it.

Beverly gave me the book Into Africa, the Epic Adventures of Stanley and Livingstone by Martin Dugard. She had read it when she was traveling to Africa and found it very interesting. It is about these two famous men written in a novel form. I gave it to her father when I got back to

Washington. I read quite a bit of it on the bus back to Livingstone and finished it in the first two days back in Windhoek. I have read other accounts of their adventures but this is the best I've read. It was especially fascinating since I know a bit more about Africa now.

These are some observations I made as we rode along. Many people were walking on paths at the edge of fields early in the morning, no doubt, going to work. There were many small roadside stands; some on mats, rugs, or blankets selling fruits, veggies, maize, and handmade objects of art. The trees I saw were mango, papaya, banana, avocado, apple and orange. The gardens included lettuce, spinach, tomatoes, carrots, beans, sweet potatoes, maize and probably other plants. Women walked from the river carrying pails of water on their heads. We went through a number of villages with "squatter type" settlements with small, what looked to be, one or two room homes with metal roofs, although sometimes they were thatched. In the country were cement block homes and some native *kraals*. At times there were open thatched huts for selling a variety of merchandise.

Two boys, one about 13 or 14 and the other 7 or 8 years old sat by me in the same seat. They ate plain white bread and apple juice and the younger one had a rice dish which they had brought. I offered them my chocolate cookies (which I really didn't need) but they said, "No, thank you." We arrived back in Livingstone about 2:15 PM. I thought we would be later with all the stops made to pick up and let off passengers. There were a few stops out in the country with no homes or footpaths around. Passengers just appeared out of the bush with their bags and parcels. Upon alighting from the bus, I had to run the gauntlet of young men wanting to carry my bag, "Mama or Meme" as they say it, but this time I knew where I was going, first to the post office and then to the Maramba Lodge and I knew where the taxis were. The driver said 35,000 kwasha but I told him I paid 20,000 before, so we settled for 25,000K, about $5.00 U.S. which they still make money on, but I figure they need it worse than I do. I'm willing to pay a fair price for anything but I don't want to be "schnookered" which happened a few times when I didn't have the right money and didn't know the language. Many of the taxi drivers don't speak English. Zambia, Botswana, and Zimbabwe all have English as the official language, as does Namibia and the signs are all in English which helps greatly.

When checking in this time at the Maramba Lodge, the receptionist told me the Chobe Park trip in Botswana was confirmed; the pickup time would be 7:15 AM. A representative came to get my $185 payment, which is high, but is supposed to be worth it. I was told by several people that I would see groups of animals, not just two to six that I had been seeing. I was assigned to Tent 8 this time but I liked #1 better because it was closer to reception, the lounge and the dining room but it was fine. It had the same configuration and facilities.

Chobe National Park-Botswana

Once again, it was an early rise for Chobe Park and once again the other five in the group were staying in one of the expensive hotels, The Falls. Irwin and Susan were from New York and Stan, David and Margie live in South Africa. The latter were showing their long-time friends around the southern part of the continent but I don't think they included Namibia in their plans. It was an hour's drive to the Botswana border. When we approached it, there was an extremely long line of trucks waiting to cross the border and on the other side of the Zambezi River there was an equally long line waiting to cross to Zambia. There is one ferry boat which holds one of these long trucks with its trailer to ferry all these trucks across the river one at a time. Some trucks wait for a week to make the crossing. This happened because of the unsettling situation in Zimbabwe which caused hijacking, stealing, some killings, and very high entrance fees, so the truckers would rather line up and wait than go through that situation.

Our van driver helped us through the departure process and the immigration procedure. He met the transport on the other side which was an outboard 10 to 12 passenger motor boat that took about five minutes to cross the Zambezi River. They, the taxi drivers, can't cross the border but can help you through the border to reliable transport on the other side. It is all prearranged. I found this to be the case when I went to Zimbabwe to take the plane back to Windhoek. This way the tourist doesn't have "to run the gauntlet" every time.

When we were getting acquainted on the boat and asking where I was from (they all knew each other) I said as I usually did, "I'm a volunteer teacher living in Namibia this year, but from the Seattle area in Washington, grew up in Ohio, lived in the Bay Area in CA for many years before moving to Washington when our two sons moved there." This was my usual spiel. Irwin asked, "Where in Ohio?" to which I replied, "Near Dayton and outside the small town of West Milton." He said, "I know where West Milton is because I traveled a lot in Ohio with the steel business." I replied with amazement, "I can't believe this, that I would be crossing the Zambezi River from Zambia to Botswana and meet someone from New York that would actually know where West Milton, Ohio is." As the saying goes, "It's a small world!" I think the five of them are very wealthy but they were friendly and accepted me into their group. There was a large number of people on this particular tour, the majority being American in the group, but the five of us kind of "hung together" during the day. At the entrance to Botswana we had to go through immigration again but it was simple and there was no visa fee.

All of us were taken to a big lodge where we boarded a big boat for the morning tour. I was a little disappointed with this since I had been on the small boat in Zambia where we could get really close to the shore, but it was part of the "package". We did see a number of animals including several different species of birds, small fresh water crocodiles, a minotaur lizard, elephants, hippos in and out of the water, about a dozen "deer animals"-eland, kudu and 'bok', warthogs, Egyptian eagles, snake birds, and Cape buffalo. There was tea, coffee, cold drinks, cookies and cakes on board. I think the majority of the tourists were senior citizen Americans from the U.S. with their new safari outfits on, trousers, shirts, hats, and shoes. Many of the women had three or four diamond and gold rings on their fingers. There were English, Germans, South Africans and some Asians plus a few younger people but not many. It was a pleasant ride because the weather was so nice. We spent most of the time on the upper deck where we could see everything very well.

After about two hours we docked back at the lodge and were treated to a very extensive buffet luncheon. My table mates only eat kosher food which Margie had brought from South Africa. They had their own paper plates, plastic utensils and glasses. Stan wears the little black cap but Irwin just had on a baseball type cap. Stan is probably 20 or more years older than Margie, very much over-weight with a fringe of white hair while Margie is tall slender and statuesque. David, their son, is average height with long dark hair. He had just graduated from secondary school and was enrolled at Brown University in the States for the fall term. They were kind of a different looking family but seemed very happy. Irwin is overweight with a fringe of gray hair and Susan has gray/white hair and a bit overweight.

After lunch we boarded the open air safari vehicles for the land tour. There were a number of elephants on land and down on the beach. They travel in families, I believe. Two hippos were sunning themselves lying on the road. I was surprised to see this because in the 5th grade science text, it was stated that if they are out in the sun they get sunburned, get sick and die. The driver did go around them but they arose and ambled back down to the river. Other groups we saw were giraffes, Cape buffalo, springbok, baboons, zebras, warthogs, guinea fowl, bushbok and others I haven't mentioned.

About 4:00 PM we started back to Livingstone and did everything in reverse. We had to pay the $50 visa fee again upon entering Zambia; the other one didn't count that I had bought less than two weeks before. The truck ferry was crossing this time so we had a really good look at it; this was very interesting to see. I think there were perhaps two automobiles on it with the truck and its very long trailer. Margie said this ferry would be the last one today because the border closes at 6:00 PM. My "five safari mates" were able to see the entrance to my lodge this time because I was let off first. The road into Maramba Lodge is dirt and was quite rutted because of the recent rains which were out of season but it was at least dry by now. I said good-bye to these very nice people when we arrived back at the lodge and thanked them for accepting me into their group. The entrances to the three fancy expensive hotels are paved, of course, with a nice brick design as you get closer to the entrance and everything is beautifully manicured and landscaped with many kinds of beautiful trees. The Maramba entrance has a lot of natural vegetation and I thought was just as pretty in a rustic type way.

That evening I had a very tasty soup and fresh fruit with ice cream for dinner. I did get that dessert in Namibia when it was available when I was eating out. It was a "big treat" for me. That night I was able to see a number of stars even with the pole lights and a three-quarter moon. I have yet to see a star laden sky like my late husband and I saw a number of years ago when we were on a cruise in Fiji out to some practically deserted islands. In my Ondangwa home I didn't go out at night even though there was an armed guard on the premises. I didn't want to take any chances.

A Brief Visit to Zimbabwe

Next morning I repacked once again and somehow stuffed everything in. I did spend a little time on the internet as I was able to do most days. No one else seemed to be using it. It was 10,000 kwasha for 20 minutes and 20,000 for 40 minutes. The taxi took me to the Zimbabwe border for 50,000 K, about $9.00 U.S. It only took about ten minutes so I probably paid too much but he did help me out at the border. This was the Zimbabwe side of Victoria Falls which is better viewing because the entire falls is visible from there and there are almost always rainbows, I was told. I saw the falls as we were approaching the border but it was a bit misty; I could feel the spray when I left the taxi. The taxi driver took me to the departure building, stayed with me there, and then walked with me across the border to meet the other taxi driver who took me to immigration where I had to pay a $35 visa fee.

I learned that I had to trust the taxi drivers because they were helpful about telling me exactly what I had to do when crossing a border, staying with me, getting me through in a minimum amount of time and delivering me safely to the other side to their friend who does the same thing with that border. This way I didn't have to go through all the hawkers by myself; since the drivers did this it was probably worth the extra money they charge. I had read there wasn't a visa fee to go into Zimbabwe, but found out differently. I suppose everyone has to get their "piece of the pie". There were trucks lined up on both sides of the border here but not nearly as many as at the Botswana/Zambia border.

The taxi ride was $40 U.S. which I thought was pretty steep but it was about a 25 or 30 minute ride to the airport. I just thought the airport would be at the edge of the town of Victoria Falls but, no, it was way out in the country. The part of Zimbabwe that we went through is very green with lots of vegetation as there was in Zambia and Botswana in comparison to Namibia. There are no towns or villages and very few homes between the town and the airport. The taxi driver didn't know why the airport was located that far from the town.

Zimbabwe uses U.S. dollars and South African rand as currency. Because their inflation went "sky high" during the recent unsettled times and their money went up into the millions and billions, they suspended it. They won't take any credit cards because they don't have the mechanism for this. I was going to buy some more postcards of Victoria Falls but they were $2.00 each so thought better of it. I learned later that some of my younger colleagues did go to the Zimbabwe side of Victoria Falls, stayed in a hostel there, met other tourists, were treated very well and experienced no problems at all. We had been cautioned against going to that country.

The airport is small but modern and was somewhat busy while I was there. There are only two gates. Most of the departing passengers were senior citizens departing from their safari holidays bidding good-bye to the others who would depart at a later time. There were a few business people going on the flights. When I went through security, the officer found two knives in my purse, the Swiss army type, which I had forgotten about.

Actually I couldn't remember where I had put them because that purse had so many pockets. I thanked him for finding them He let me put them in my checked baggage which was on a little trailer in the room next door. I should have given him one of them but didn't think of that until later. I had a bottle of water, also, but they weren't concerned about that. When I told him I was a volunteer teacher living in Namibia this year etc., but now on holiday, he became very friendly and was interested in what I was saying. He thanked me for doing this.

Back to Windhoek, Namibia

The plane to Windhoek, Namibia was small and held about twenty four passengers; I think it was a turbo prop. The flight was about three hours long. It stopped in Maun, Botswana for about thirty minutes to pick up eight more people, actually there were nine that boarded the plane, and so after the pilot checked the manifold twice once we boarded, calling their names, one lady had to get off, reluctantly, I might add. When we had reboarded the plane, on our seats was a boxed meal which contained meatloaf, a roll, small veggie salad, fruit, cake and a bottle of water. There is no flight attendant. I ate half of the meal and finished the other half when I arrived at the hotel in Windhoek. There is a one-hour time difference between the two countries since Namibia went on daylight savings in April. This lasted until the first Sunday of September; I didn't know about it in April until I went to school at 7:30 AM, the usual time, and hardly anyone was there and about a half hour later staff and learners came "dribbling" in; then I was told, "Oh, yes, for the winter we start an hour later." Back to the flight, it was rather routine but then became a bit bumpy. At one point, the windshield was covered with ice and frost as we were going through the clouds. We could see into the cockpit. I don't think the pilots could see anything. I was hoping they could fly by instruments and I was wondering if it was time for us to be saying our "Hail Marys"? My apologies to the Catholics, please. As we flew closer to Windhoek and descended through the clouds the ice did melt and visibility was better.

At the airport I didn't have any problem going through immigration since I was living in Namibia that year, however since there were very few passengers coming in, they had no problems either. The Steiner Guesthouse where I was staying for a week arranged transport from the airport. I didn't see my name on any of the cards being held up by drivers. I wandered around for a bit inside and outside, then a very presentable man came up to me and gave me a message that he had been in contact with "my driver" who was having car trouble so he was to take me to the hotel because they exchanged taxi passengers sometimes. He must have heard me say Steiner, so I went with him, finding out when I arrived at the hotel that he had "fed me a line" so I learned another lesson, I hope; he overcharged me as well. The real driver had had a flat tire but went to the airport and found me not there. Everything turned out all right. This driver was very friendly and we talked all the way into Windhoek which is a 30-35 minute drive. We went through a very heavy thunder, lightning and rain storm which is unheard of at this time of the year in that area. There were reports of heavy hailstorms in a few parts of Windhoek which is a rarity as well.

My stay at the hotel for a week before going to the Back Packers Unite Hostel for our mid-service meeting for World Teach was pleasant and restful and I accomplished what I had planned to do. I spent time making arrangements for Brad's, one of my sons, visit to Namibia in late August/ early September, orienting myself to the city, buying some items that aren't available up north, going to the internet café most days, reading writing, and relaxing in the courtyard by the pool. It is a tropical setting with palm, orange, banana and other trees. Some were quite large and looked to be very old. It was warm enough for sunbathing but I didn't see anyone in the pool. The weather was quite cool in the morning and evening because winter was approaching but was warm during most of the daytime.

I wasn't really looking forward to the mid-service meeting particularly because it meant more meetings and more strategies for teaching and coping with culture shock which we had been inundated with several times over, but it was nice to see all the people in our group once again, some of which I hadn't seen since January but others I had seen from time to time up in the northern area. One night we were entertained by a group of young adult dancers with their singing and dancing. They were certainly energetic and seemed to be having a lot of fun while performing. This was very enjoyable. Their program lasted for about two hours.

One day during the lunch break, a few of us went to visit an orphanage several blocks away from the hostel. Heidi, one of the volunteer's (Rachel) mother, had come to visit her and help out for three months. She had made contact with the director, somehow in the States, over the internet and was invited to visit this orphanage which has children from parents who have died from AIDS. Heidi's husband is a family physician in Wisconsin where they live. The family is very aware of people's needs and acts upon their beliefs in this area. At the orphanage there were probably thirty children from the ages of 2 to 13 or 14. It really was heartbreaking to see them but the children were very friendly, loving and seemed happy. Heidi had bought many bags of groceries and some toys for the children. She had visited there the day before. I didn't take my camera because I thought it might be intrusive but Rachel had hers and she and Heidi were snapping pictures like crazy. I asked Rachel if she would e-mail me a few. The directors told us there are seven children who are HIV-positive and they receive the medicine every day. The others are tested periodically to see if they have the disease. The young man who started the orphanage was a street kid, got into drugs but then turned his life around and wanted to do something for other children so this is the result. He just depends on private donations; the government doesn't help at all.

On Sunday we came back to our schools by bus. This time we had a huge bus, eight people, and not very much baggage. One never knows what will turn up. Also, this time the bus arrived at the hostel at 6:20 AM instead of 7:45 AM–unheard of in Africa–and we were told to get ready fast, grab a bite to eat (which Evelyn and I did) but the younger people who weren't up yet took their time lining up for the shower, fixing a leisurely breakfast and then bringing their bags out. We were all ready by 7:45 except for one of the girls and she came out with her boyfriend who was going on other transportation at 8:30 AM.

All good times have to come to an end, as this one did, but I was very happy that I had the opportunity to see all the things I saw. Some people asked if I went alone, which I did. I do prefer traveling with someone so I have someone with which to share experiences, but if I have no one to go with me, I will go alone, and this one I had to plan myself. IT WAS WORTH IT!!!

February and March flooding at Heroes School

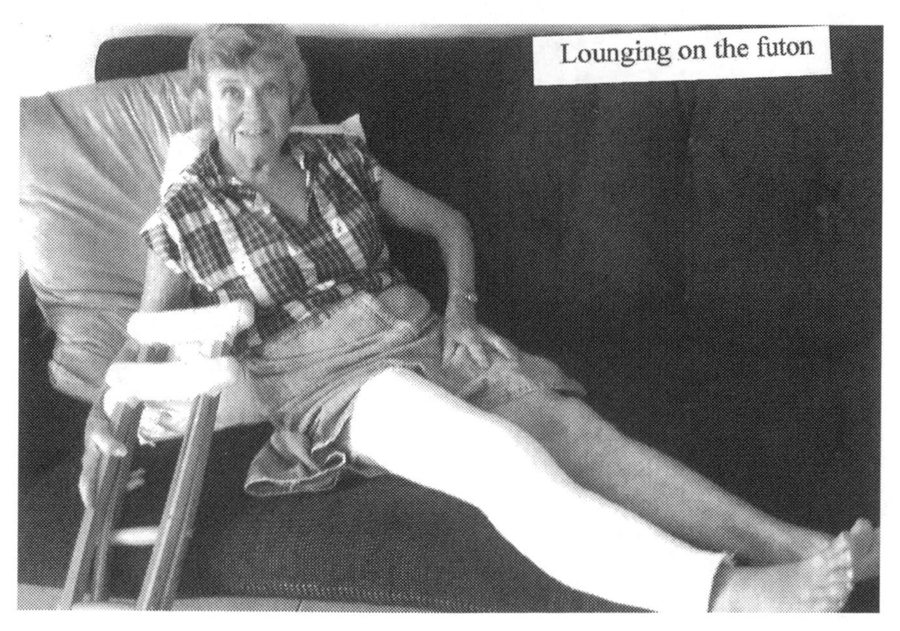

Norene lounging on the futon

Learners at morning assembly

At an open meat market in Ondangwa

The mighty Victoria Falls, Zambia side

National Science Fair winners-Grade 5

Feeding "Big Danny" at Mosi-oa-Tunya National Park, Zambia

A TRIP TO NORTHWEST NAMIBIA

Chapter 13--June 13 to 16, 2009

June 16 is the Day of the African Child. It commemorates an event which happened on June 16, 1976 when hundreds of black school children in Soweto, South Africa were massacred and thousands were injured by the racist regime when protesting against the inferior education in their schools. There had been previous protests but because TV coverage was more prominent at this time, it was widely covered and the picture of a man carrying the body of Hector Pieterson, who had been shot and killed, with his grieving sister running along beside them, was shown around the world. This brought attention of the situation to the entire world community. I was able to visit the Hector Pieterson Museum later on when I was in Johannesburg. I was told there were some programs in some of the cities to remember this; there were none up in my area to my knowledge. This created a four-day weekend for the schools. Actually it was almost five days because some schools did not meet on Friday at all. Heroes was dismissed at 10:30 AM. When I asked one of the staff why this was, they said, "because it is a four day weekend." I suppose this makes sense; if we have four days off, why not five? My learners didn't seem to know the significance of the holiday.

Evelyn and I took this opportunity to go to the northwest to see that area. She arranged for us to rent a car, actually a five passenger Toyota truck from Avis, and have one of her young friends Elia, who teaches at another school near her, drive it. He speaks several of the native languages of Namibia which helped greatly. His friend Murphy went along "in case they had to change a flat tire" he said. On Saturday morning two of our World Teach colleagues from other schools rode up with us since they had planned to go to the town of Opuwo, our first major stop, to visit some other World Teach volunteers who are living and teaching there.

After leaving Oshakati, the nearest larger town to Ondangwa, and traveling west, the area was noticeably different because of less vegetation and more flat land, as well as less homes and people. There were many more donkeys, cattle and goats. Donkeys are used as beasts of burden here, as I've mentioned before. Elia chose to take a short cut that he heard about which would cut off 100 kilometers. Outside of one of the small towns, we visited the birthplace of Namibia's first president, Sam Nujoma, "the George Washington of Namibia", Elia said. There were still some of the *kraal* huts in the fenced compound but several other concrete or brick buildings had been included. We weren't allowed to take any pictures. One quite elderly gentleman was sitting outside; he was President Nujoma's brother, we think; it was difficult to understand him even for Elia.

The shortcut road was dirt but a good one especially since it had been very dry since the summer storms were over. It was an interesting drive through this Himba cattle and goat grazing country. At one point there were many of these animals at a watering place. The water was pumped up from an underground well, stored in an overhead tank and then pumped into the troughs. It was interesting to note how the animals waited patiently for their turn to drink. We did see several other watering places during the next few days.

The next two paragraphs are paraphrased from The Lonely Planet guide book. "The Himba tribe has been the widely photographed subject of many travel brochures and coffee table books because they still follow many of the customs of their forefathers. The women have the practice of smearing red ochre mixed with a little melted butter on their bodies to make their skin smooth and 'young' looking. They are bare breasted, have elaborate braided hairdos, wear short leather skirts with big ruffles in the back and adorn themselves with a lot of jewelry. The men wear loin cloths and have one or two very thick braids on top of their heads with the rest of the head clean shaven. Some of the men wear western clothing and perhaps some of the women do; I'm not sure about this.

The other prominent tribe in this area is the Herero. These women have very distinctive attire different from the Himba. Their dress is derived from the Victorian-era German missionaries. It consists of an enormous crinoline worn over a series of petticoats with a horn-shaped hat or headdress. On

August 23rd thousands of Herero turn out in traditional dress to honor their fallen chiefs on Maherero Day."

In the early afternoon we dropped Lindsey and James off at Carmen's school and residence. Another of the young women volunteers was staying with her because of some trouble at her school residence out in the country about twelve kilometers away. Carmen's boyfriend is in the same town but living in another part of town and teaching at another school. We all had a nice chat together then Elia and Murphy dropped us off at our hotel and went to find their place to stay. The Okahane Hotel is a nice budget type motel with a tropical setting in the courtyard. I may have mentioned before that many homes and businesses are walled, fenced, gated and locked to the outside and almost all of the businesses have one or more guards at the entrance and inside because of the likely possibility of thievery.

After settling into the room for a bit, we went walking around the town which isn't very big. It was quieting down because most of the stores and businesses close between 1:00 and 2:00 PM on Saturday for the weekend. There were the Himba and Herero people and others along the streets. The Herero wear beautiful dresses and it was interesting to see all the different colors and fabrics. At first, it was unusual to see the bare-breasted Himba women but it becomes more common the more one sees them. I did get a few pictures of the "locals". The procedure is to ask first to take a photo and if they consent, they will tell how much it will cost.

About 5:30 PM we drove up a very dusty, windy and bumpy dirt road to the Country House which is a very nice restaurant overlooking a valley to the mountains on the other side. People go there to view the sunset which wasn't very spectacular this evening since there were no clouds. We met some more of our colleagues from World Teach and had a great time together. There were thirteen of us including Elia and Murphy. There was a pool there, where the water just flows over the edge and falls to where, I don't know? Some of the group stayed for dinner but we had told the hotel we would have dinner back there. Four of the group told us they would see us in Epupa Falls the next day as they were planning to go there as well.

Next morning we did leave for the Epupa Falls which is at the northern border of Namibia; across the Kunene River " a long stone's throw" away is Angola. It was a long journey on an undulating dirt road of six to seven hours with our stops. Along the way there were the cattle and goats being herded through the grazing areas by the Himba boys and girls. At times we had to stop for them to clear the road. There was a sign at the entrance to a Himba Primary school; we decided to turn in. This was Sunday of the four-day weekend but the teacher, Ruana, was there with her three children. She invited us to see the one-room school where fifty-five learners, grades 1 through 4 meet. There were many charts/posters on the wall including alphabet picture/letter cards, maps, number charts, children's work and tribal language lists. She said some of the classes meet out under the trees; I would think so because 55 children could not fit into that one room even with the very few tables and benches. Ruana is the only teacher for these children. After grade 4 they go to a public school some distance away.

She asked if we would like to visit their village and, of course, we did. We were hoping to visit a Himba village. It was just a short distance back in a field away from the school. Elia drove back; we waited outside the fence of the compound while she went in to ask if it was permissible for us to go in. She beckoned us in. First we met one of the sixty year old twin brothers who are the heads of the family, somewhat like a chief. (This is my term for them.) One has three wives and the other has four. We were told that we could take pictures. Each wife has her own hut for herself and her children, I believe. Ruana led us around the large circle of huts; some were made of closely set poles and grasses while others had clay and red ochre mud walls with mostly thatched roofs. The women and children were friendly and seemed to enjoy having their pictures taken, then were eager to see them on the window of the digital camera. We were invited into one hut where a young woman was slathering the red ochre mixture on her body. She didn't seem to mind our watching her and taking photographs. The children seemed especially eager to see us and they were all so beautiful; I wanted to embrace all of them.

Our circle tour ended back at the men's hut where there were handcrafts laid out on mats for us to buy. Evelyn bought a Himba doll and I bought a small drum; I would have bought a doll but the other one was rather ugly, I thought, but I did buy one later at another place which was better looking. When we left, Elia gave Ruana gifts to give to them of sugar, tobacco, pocket knives and some small toys for the children. He and Evelyn had discussed taking gifts to give if we did get to visit a Himba village. We gave him money to buy the things because he knew what was appropriate.

Next Ruana asked if we were interested in seeing some dancing; there was a group having a three day celebration not far from where we were. Of course we wanted to see this. Down the road about four kilometers away, the group was assembled under four trees; the women and children were sitting under three trees and the men were a bit farther away under another tree. As we walked in we shook hands with and greeted some of the women on the way to the men. Ruana introduced us to the oldest man whom she said was the "owner" of the tribe. She and Elia conversed with him inquiring if we would be able to see them dance. After a bit of discussion with the other men he said, "Yes, for $100 Nam." This is about $12 U.S. We paid him; he went over to the groups sitting under the trees apparently telling them what was happening.

Shortly six of the younger women arose, got in a line and started singing, swaying and clapping; then others followed forming a semi-circle with the men on one side and the women on the other. The men and women took turns jumping into the center of the circle and dancing quite vigorously. At times they danced to the other side and made motions to hit someone but didn't actually touch the person. One lady said the dance was about killing a cow. This may or may not be true, I don't know. They were singing and clapping all the time during the dancing. They seemed to be really enjoying themselves and we were having a great time watching all of this. After about thirty minutes we took our leave, thanking everyone profusely. (One can never say too many thank yous.) Elia and Ruana talked to the "owner" and gave them gifts, the same as we did for the little village conclave and we were on our way once again. We stopped at an interesting little Herero graveyard by the side of the road in which the stones had several cow horns as part of the marker. We learned later that the more horns there are the more important the person is and for men the horn tips are pointing up and for women they point downward.

In mid-afternoon we had our first glimpse of Epupa Falls in the distance and then went down into this tropical valley with many palm trees and other large trees including a few baobab trees. It is a beautiful area and so much different than the Ondangwa area. There aren't a lot of buildings there but those that are there are down by the river. I mentioned before that the Kunene River flows between the northern Namibian and southern Angolan borders here. Our chalet which faced the very calm river was shaped like a safari tent but had a solid floor, walls and ceiling. The large windows were screened and had pull-up canvas shades. The bathroom had a shower with beautiful rock walls and floor-open with no door or curtain. In the middle of the room was a very large rectangular rock "bench". The room was quite unique and interesting.

Anthony, manager of the lodge, was very helpful and knew a lot about the area regarding flora, fauna, geography and directions to different parts of Namibia. He, his wife and small daughter Kira, have been there for three years. He is hoping to own it in seven more. They are from Germany originally but really like the Epupa Falls area. It is beautiful but so far away from any other place with a settlement. They go to Swakopmund on the central coast for their holidays.

After freshening up and unpacking a bit, we headed for the falls which was only a short distance away. There we met two of the World Teach group, Jen and Erica, who had come with Chris and Chloe. The four of them had settled into the campground. The young people do travel as much as they can but they go the really budget way because they do not have an extra income, but they have a lot of fun. I told them that I had earned my "lodge stay" after teaching for 31 years, but I would have gone camping too, if I had had a car and the equipment. Epupa Falls is horseshoe shaped with a lot of water flowing over the rocks since there had been such heavy rain falls in the summer of January, February and March. It is an impressive sight. While we were standing there admiring the beauty of the whole scene, Chris and Chloe came back from a hike further up and told us to go further up the hill to see many more falls cascading down from the hillsides particularly on the Angola side. We did do this the next morning. Each time we were at this particular part of the falls there were always a few women washing clothes on the rocks by one of the smaller tributaries flowing into the larger river.

The dining room was open-air with a gentle breeze blowing through. The air was warmer at night up here than down where I lived. There were a few other people in the dining room besides Evelyn and me. Breakfast and dinner were included in the price of the room probably because there was no other place to get a meal. On the second night the dining room was nearly full. I was surprised to find the number of people who had made their way to this rather remote spot. Kudu was featured on the menu the first night and braised ox tail on the second. The meal was served buffet style after the appetizer; and there were two meat selections, two vegetables besides potatoes, some kind of rice or pasta and a salad. Dessert was served at the table afterwards. The meal was quite ample and so was breakfast. There was afternoon tea each day, as well.

On our second day, Owen, a sixteen year old boy, led the hike up the hill passing the main falls and down the other side to a very sandy beach. On the way there and back, we were able to see the numerous waterfalls cascading down the hills on the far side of the river, the Angolan side. It was a beautiful sight! When we reached the beach area, it was very quiet, calm and peaceful, much different than in the falls area. We sat on some large lava rocks and soaked up the silence. On the way back to the lodge,

Owen had us stop at each of the view points for another look at the scene. He was a very knowledgeable guide. Elia had become friends with him the day before and suggested he go with us. He asked for $80 but we gave him $100.

For lunch we had planned a picnic in the campground for the four of us and had bought some supplies before leaving Opuwo-some ribs, steaks, bread, potato salad, strawberries, bananas, and charcoal. This plan turned into something else as things there seem to have a habit of doing. Elia asked if we would like to go to a nice park about seven kilometers away where there were big trees and picnic benches and meet another tribe living in that area. This sounded interesting so we agreed. He and Murphy were staying up the hill where several families lived. I don't know if they had known them before or just made friends upon arriving. They were both very sociable and made friends very easily. We went back up there to get some of the things we had brought with us. The manager of the lodge had kept some of our items in the fridge at the lodge until we needed them. Two young women and a boy were going with us as well, so Elia bought some goat meat from a woman who was cutting off pieces from a carcass that was hanging on a hook in one of the open air huts. He bought some freshly baked Himba bread as well.

Finally after some more waiting and moving around (no hurrying) of some of the folk, we were off down another dirt road. It quickly became a very rocky road, I think rougher than any trail or forest road that I've ever been on. The truck was traveling along in the two ruts for vehicles and we were being shaken and jostled quite vigorously. Evelyn and I were becoming increasingly concerned about damage to the truck since we were financially responsible for it. She did buy insurance for the trip but it didn't cover everything. Elia had backed into something the day before leaving a small dent and scratch in the bumper; it wasn't anything big but we all know how rental car companies are about those things. We both said, "This is not a good idea," but he kept driving, saying the place was "just down there a little bit farther." We couldn't get out of the ruts to turn around.

A little bit farther along, Evelyn told him to stop at the next flat area for the *braai* (barbeque); he did this. It was a nice spot with a number of trees and the river was just down a small hill. We had gone four or five kilometers; I could have sworn it was ten miles. Elia built a fire pit with some of the rocks while Monica, a very pushy young lady who squeezed in at the last minute, marinated the meat. Finally it was cooked-very well done which made it tough. I had about two bites with some bread then went to get some potato salad but the spoons that were put in the cooler when we bought it were gone and, of course, no one could tell what happened to them. This happens frequently there; things disappear and no one has a clue as to how it happened. There was no fruit but we did have drinks so the *braai* turned out reasonably well. I was thinking that at tea time later in the afternoon, I could get something else to eat, if I was hungry. I was not looking forward to the trip back over the same road but it did seem shorter than when we went, as it happens sometimes.

That evening we drove to a point up on the hill to view all the falls and the sunset in the opposite direction which wasn't outstanding because there were no clouds but it was a pleasant experience. Elia told us our "out time" would be at 6:00 AM the next morning. At 6:00 AM he was at the gate of the lodge to pick us up. He drove back up the hill to get Murphy plus six learners whom we were taking back to their boarding school some distance away. There was much bustling about by children and adults; we were on our way about 6:45 AM which is pretty good by Namibian standards. After traveling for about an hour Elia stopped the truck; he and Murphy had a quiet discussion and then said they had forgotten to put in the spare tire, so there was nothing to do but go back for it. They had taken it out while getting the children in with all their gear which made the back quite full, so this added two extra hours to the trip.

On the way back to Opuwo, after leaving the learners off at their school, when Elia was driving down one of the hills (a little too fast, I think) the truck stopped very quickly when hitting one of the little ravines which had been made during the rainy season. Evelyn and I both flew up hitting our heads and backs on the roof of the car. I know now what instantaneous means because this happened in a split second. We didn't have the seatbelts fastened because of getting lax about this after riding in the taxis, where usually it was hard to find them, so it was our fault. The men had their belts fastened so this didn't happen to them. Evelyn was really moaning and groaning; I hurt some but not badly. The guys were very concerned about us. There was a man lying in the back of the truck whom we had given a ride after leaving the children off; he went up and hit the roof as well and was hurting. Thank God the children were not still in the car. This put a damper on the trip. I felt pretty good but I could tell that Evelyn didn't, but she didn't complain very much; she is a "trouper".

In Opuwo we stopped to get petrol and Elia took the injured man someplace, we didn't know where. While they did this, Evelyn and I went back to the hotel where we had stayed to get some coffee and a snack. The breakfast buffet was still laid out for some other customers so we took some bread and cheese from there to have with our coffee. When we went over to the office to pay, after a little discussion the two ladies there said they weren't going to charge us anything for this which we thought was quite nice of them.

The trip back to Ondangwa was rather uneventful but this was fine with us because we had done and seen all the things we had hoped to see and do; there was no need to make long stops. The truck was returned to Avis by 3:00 PM after being washed and vacuumed. We did have to pay extra for the scratch in the bumper, but apparently that fiercely bumpy ride didn't damage the vehicle. The charge for the damage to the bumper was almost as much as we had paid to rent the car. I don't know what the insurance we'd bought paid for, but apparently **not much**. We were told that the company would have to send the truck to Windhoek to have it repaired. What a crock, but we couldn't do anything else but pay the extra! All in all we enjoyed the four-day holiday and so did the guys. Murphy said, "he got lucky". It was a free trip for them but Elia did have to do all the driving and he was a good driver; we did compensate him, of course.

One sad note for me was that Evelyn decided to go back to Washington, D.C., where she lives, for some medical treatment due to the accident, which she wasn't sure of getting here. She had gone back to the doctor to be examined and got more pain pills which helped, but she didn't want to depend on them. A week or so later, she did go to the private hospital to be x-rayed and was told she should go to Windhoek or Cape Town to be further examined. This was when she decided to go home. I really missed her because we had gotten together every weekend but I could certainly understand and support her decision. She left Ondangwa on July 3rd, flew to Windhoek and then back to her home a few days later. When she was examined by her own doctor it was found that she had a broken vertebra. She did recover from that and was feeling very well after several weeks.

My younger colleagues told me to contact them more often for a get-together. I did spend that weekend with them at our favorite hotel in Ongwediva where we celebrated the 4th of July. I invited John Carlo to meet us there because he had been wanting to meet some other volunteers--I think younger ones is what he meant although he never said that. We just talked, ate, and drank our refreshments mostly and were happy just being able to "let our hair down" and vent on some of our mutual challenges. We could laugh and complain about things without it going any further.

Some of the group went to a late night concert on Saturday night after our pizza party and found that it was **really** late. It was supposed to start at 10:00 PM but they left at 2:00 AM when it still hadn't started. Africa time was "alive and well." I remember when I was in Kenya years earlier, one of our guest speakers said, "The time for an event is when it happens." How true! There was another overnight gathering a few weeks later at one of the couples' homes which I had planned to attend but that was the only time during the year when I didn't feel very well with a bad throat, so I didn't go.

CAN YOU BORROW ME A PEN, MISS NORENE?

Chapter 14--July & August, 2009

Can you borrow me a pen, Miss Norene? This is a question I heard almost daily; it is the Namibian way of asking to borrow something. I tried to teach the learners the correct way of asking to borrow something but I knew I wouldn't change their ways because this is the way adults talk. When someone "borrows them something" often this is the last the lender will ever see it again. After a time, I made them give me a shoe so they would return it. Some of them seemed to think this was the craziest thing they had ever heard and **would not** hand over the shoe; they didn't see the connection. They would have rather gone without the pen than do this. I really didn't need the pen back because I took a lot of pens with me, but I wanted them to think of taking responsibility for what they needed at school. After a time, some did give the shoe. I asked some 7th graders if they have the word, *loan or lend*, in their language; they said that a loan is when you borrow money from the bank. Some of the teachers started joking with me, when they heard of this, asking if they needed to give me a shoe when they wanted to borrow something.

Another Namibian expression is with the "*nows*". If they say they will do something "now", it most likely will be in the distant future or never. Two "*nows*", e.g. "*now, now*" means it will get done but sometime later, where as three *nows*, "*now, now, now*" means right now! I began to use this quite often regarding assignments that needed to be finished.

School was moving right along since the seventh month was now completed. The time did go by rather quickly. One disappointment I had during Term 2 was that I was assigned two student teachers for my Grade 5 and Grade 7 Science classes when I felt I was really getting a handle on things and learning all of their names. Eight of these young people from a nearby teachers' college came on the first day of Term 2 and were in the classroom teaching one week later. I could readily see why a number in the classes couldn't write a complete sentence correctly because my student teachers had very basic mistakes in their writing on charts and summaries on the chalkboard for the learners to copy. They would be going into the classrooms to teach the next year so the level of English continues where it is. There was very little classroom control. I know they have to learn how to teach somehow but it was really painful for me to watch this. One of them did seem interested in teaching Science but the other was just in it for the money she would make, I felt. I was supposed to observe and critique them which I did. They listened nicely and then did pretty much what they wanted. Their teacher from the college came a few times during the term; I did talk to her about my observations but I was never asked to write an evaluation which I had expected. I had one written for each but never had a chance to turn it in. I did still have my Grade 5 English class and I felt that I made real headway there. I've always been a "stickler" for correct spelling and I saw so many misspelled words; I saw this in the regular teachers' work as well at times. I know it is their second language and English is a difficult language to learn but they have been at it for quite awhile since English has been the official language for almost twenty years. I was asked at times by teachers and students to edit something they wanted to have printed and I did enjoy helping out in this way

Early in the term before the four day holiday, I invited my Grade 5 class to my home to watch me make Peanut Biscuits, a Malawi recipe. It was in the English book as an example of getting information from reading. The whole class did fit in my living room/kitchen combination room, all thirty-seven of them. I had made enough biscuits ahead of time so they would each have two but did make the recipe explaining measurements and following the recipe which I had written on a chart which was posted up on the wall. I felt like "Julia Child" except I wasn't sipping wine as I was working. They were all very good and listened attentively. I made a drink for them and said that if anyone spilled their drink, it would be his/her responsibility to clean it up. Someone did, Kandiwapa; he came up to me and asked if I had a mop but I gave him some paper towels instead.

The learners clean their own classrooms; a committee of several sweep the room twice a day (because of the sand mostly and paper bits thrown on the floor) and the Friday crew have the job of sweeping and mopping so they know "housekeeping chores". After the recipe lesson was over, one of the girls, Selicky, offered to sweep the place, which she did and then she said she would mop it for me but I told her that wasn't necessary. I gave her some cookies I had because she was so nice to do it for me.

In May when I was in Windhoek I went to a travel agent who was recommended to me and told him what I had in mind for my December holiday after the school year was finished. He said he would get busy on it and I should check back with him in a few days which I did but he hadn't heard anything from his contact. I came back up to Ondangwa to start Term 2 and e-mailed him every few days and called him, but it was always the same story, he hadn't heard anything from the contact, so I gave up on "dear Bennie" and contacted the travel agent in Massachusetts who arranged all the World Teach flights from the States to here; she had something for me in just a few days. I knew the time was several months away but one had to start early to have something definite done when you have to do everything over the internet. Anyway, almost everything was in place for me to go to South Africa to Cape Town and Johannesburg then to Dar es Salaam, Mt. Kilimanjaro (not to climb-maybe ten years ago, I could have done it) then to Zanzibar, back to Dar es Salaam to Johannesburg to get the flight from there to Dulles Airport then to Seattle.

In July two of the teachers asked me if I was intending to sell or give away things I had bought when I would be leaving. I was expecting this but not THIS SOON, five months before I would actually leave and I told them so; they just laughed. I had thought some about this and was going to offer my neighbors in the other part of the house, Mr. and Mrs. Caparros and the two Filipino teachers who board with them, what I would leave behind because they had been so very kind and helpful to me from the very beginning. I didn't have items that were worth much except for my laptop and CD/radio player which I was going to give them, but hadn't said anything about this as yet. They were never "demanding nor actually expecting that things should be given to them" as I found some of the Namibians to be. Mr. Caparros wouldn't even take any money for petrol when he gave me rides to or from town.

When Evelyn was still there, in early June, I went to her home for the weekend to visit and to see the "Miss Winter" pageant organized by the student body. Her school has grades 8–12 with about two thirds of them being boarding learners. The event was supposed to start at 7 or 8:00 PM we were told. Some girls came to get us at 7:30 PM. Evelyn's home was on the school grounds just as mine is. When we arrived the loud booming music was already going in full gear and we were seated up in front near one of the huge speakers. There was much bustling about; the program seemed to be well organized with the eight contestants' different activities, e.g. sportswear, swim suit, speeches, evening clothes, etc. interspersed with entertainment, so the girls could change for the next event. There was a lot of "lag time" between activities. We stayed until after 10:00 PM and heard later that the program ended about 3:00 AM. The girls were all beautiful and looked terrific in all the different attire which they wore. This was another Namibian experience. I learned that many schools have a beauty pageant at some time of the year.

Late in July, the two other science teachers, Mr. David and Ms Marissa, and I went to a nearby college to a Science Fair in which nine of our learners participated with their projects they had been working on for the last few months. Our transport was in one of the teacher's pickup trucks; I think she was "volunteered" (maybe "borrowed") for the job. At any rate, we put a foam mattress from my home in the back of the truck where the two younger teachers and nine learners with their cardboard displays sat, all bundled up because it seemed colder than usual that morning and the wind was blowing stronger than usual. The temperature was probably between 40 and 45 degrees F in the morning during winter time; it did start warming up about 10:00 AM and rose to probably 75 degrees in the afternoon which was quite pleasant. Back to the truck--I got to sit up in the cab with Helen, the driver, because I'm "Meme Kuku" respected older lady, everyone's granny.

The program was scheduled to start at 8:00 AM but once again in typical African fashion, events started to get going about 9:30. The first judging was going to start at 10 AM (only one hour late) but the chief judge had not yet arrived so this had to wait until 11:00 AM when he did arrive. I think there were 12 judges, whom our science teacher, Mr. David, had trained during his sabbatical from Heroes School, who worked in groups of two for the 30+ projects. During the lunch break about 1:30 PM, some of them left for the day, so the remaining ones had to do double duty for the afternoon. I was assigned to sit with the chief judge and tally the marks; this was an easy job. One thing that bothered me was the incessant loud music that was blasting out from the very large speakers; I did go outside a few times to get away from it to "rest my ears and brain". After all the scores were in and the tallying was done, certificates were handed out to all the participants including the judges and it was learned who would go to the next level.

The following week, we had another Science Fair at our school; I was wondering how it would be and it was "Déjà vu all over again". I thought it might be a bit better because Mr. David, the head science teacher at Heroes, is efficient in many ways but it wasn't his fault that some of the learners and judges from other schools arrived 1 ½ to 2 hours late (right on schedule), so we couldn't start without all the judges. This time I was drafted into being a judge; I had a general idea of what to do because of reading the instructions the previous week and seeing the scoring but I thought it wouldn't be fair to the learners because they were actually vying to go to the National Science Fair in Windhoek in early September when Term 3 started. It all worked out fine because my partner and very good friend Marissa who taught Science 8-10 at Heroes had been one of the judges before, so I learned from her as we went along. It was interesting but very tiring. There were 33 projects altogether. We did have definite criteria to follow. It finally was over about 6:00 PM and a lot of the learners were going to National with their projects because they had "made the cut". The learners had worked very hard on designing and carrying out their projects from what I saw at our school. There was NO music which helped a lot; I had asked David about that before-hand; he knew that I don't like loud music. I hoped this was the end of science fairs that I was supposed to attend.

The competitions were held at different circuits and regions at this time. I knew I didn't want to go to the National. Three of my learners did go to Windhoek for the National Science Fair. They had done a study on HINI, swine flu, mostly on their own with text, charts and photographs. I had helped them get started on it but they did the rest using information from the internet mostly. I was very proud of them and after everything was over, I had a little ceremony in the classroom presenting certificates which I made and some little prizes. Their classmates clapped very loudly for them. The three said they would enter the Science Fair contest the next year.

Before Term 2 ended, the Heroes Staff had a "thank-you/going away" party for the student teachers who were here all during that term. For me, it was the "going away" part that I was thanking "my two" for although I did tell them I enjoyed having them and wished them good luck in their teaching career; (I told a white lie); I was not sorry to see them leave. They were pleasant and likeable but I just wanted my classes back under my control. I volunteered to be on the planning committee because I wanted to see how that operated and it was interesting. I won't go into a great deal of detail because this would take too long, but suffice to say, after a lot of discussion, shopping, and preparation, it did turn out well. Each staff member was supposed to contribute $30 (which some of them never did pay) and the learners were asked to give $1 to which I really objected, but to no avail. The menu consisted of chicken legs, foot long pieces of sausage, potato, macaroni and tossed salads, beer, wine, juice, or soda. I made 7 kg of potato salad and some chicken for my part. The water and electricity was off for several hours in the afternoon when I was making my potato salad the day before but I managed OK because I always had some water stored in a bucket and some cooking pots-just in case. My stove was gas so I could cook the potatoes. My concern mostly was about all the food and drinks that were stored in my fridge but the power and water did come on in time for everything to be alright. They used my kitchen since it was the handiest. One teacher did all the sausage on the *braai* pit. The dinner was in the hall (multi-purpose room). When everyone was seated and the prayer was given for the official start, one of the teachers explained just how much food each person was to take. For the drinks those who ordered wine had one whole bottle, "juice people" had one liter, the sodas were three cans to a person and the one man who chose beer had one six-pack of Windhoek lager. It was all very interesting and I did enjoy being on the committee because I felt that I really got to know my colleagues better working with them in a small group and being in a "non-school" situation. The party was fun and everyone seemed to enjoy themselves.

Here's a bit more about disciplinary measures in the schools. Corporal punishment has been outlawed for a number of years, since 1990, but some teachers and schools still use it, not nearly as much in my school as in others I heard about from my World Teach colleagues. There had been a lot of discussion in Namibia concerning a bill afoot about The Child Care and Protection Act. One of the staff told me early on that Heroes does not practice corporal punishment which I was happy to hear, however some of the behavior reinforcements that were used were equally as bad or worse in my judgment. If I were on the receiving end, I think I would rather have taken a few whacks on the rear than do some of the things that were occasionally meted out. The punishments usually happened in the staff room and because this is where we all sat to do our work when not in the classroom, it was hard not to see the actions that were taken. I saw one of the teachers hit several of the Grade 5 learners in the back during his/her class, really hard, when I went in for my class because it was time for me, but this person had not yet finished. I asked why this happened and the reply was that these learners hadn't done their homework and were disrupting the class. I said, "There is nothing about this in the Code of Conduct which was adopted by Heroes and sent home for all parents to sign." The response to me was, "All the punishments are not stated in the Code", but I know they are. The situation seemed to improve a little after our conflicting opinions. I know I was a guest in their country and I certainly wasn't there to change things however I thought I didn't have anything to lose by speaking up; what could happen other than my being fired but I didn't think this would happen because I was a volunteer and the owners of the school, Mr. and Mrs. Kapia, liked me. The teacher's answer to me was, "This isn't America, Ms Norene."

Another thing that bothered me was the way the African teachers laugh when a child is being punished. My Filipino friends did not do this. The student teachers laughed at them as well. One of them asked me one day, "Miss Norene, don't people in America laugh?" I replied, "Oh, yes, we do laugh at a lot of things, but we do not laugh at others misfortunes and especially when a child is being punished; this is not funny." I really don't think she got my message. Some of my learners, especially in Grade 5 said and wrote that they liked me because they knew I wouldn't beat them; isn't this a fine testimony about a teacher? I had told them that I don't believe in that; there are other ways of doing things.

A Presidential election was scheduled for November but the date had not yet been decided. I couldn't believe this!! There had been a number of rumors going around regarding when Term 3 would be over because of this. It was scheduled to be December 4. The two scenarios were: if the election were early in November, there would be a three-day vacation; I didn't know what the reason for a three-day vacation from school was because most of the learners are not of a voting age yet. The other premise was that if it were near the middle of November, Term 3 would finish before the election and that would be the end of the school year. Another rumor was that this would not be known before Term 3 started on September 8 and so things go in Namibia. This would not have interfered with any of my plans. If we did get out early, I would probably go on an organized camping trip someplace in Namibia before I took the trip that I had planned starting December 4. I realized later that the schools were going to be used as voting venues and some apparently did not have a large multi-purpose room for this, such as Heroes did, and classrooms would need to be used for the voting process.

Exams were scheduled to start in one week so this was going to be a very busy time in the schools. I mentioned before that the Ministry of Education puts so much emphasis on exams and there is a lot of time wasted in those two weeks. Apparently it has been this way for several years and even though there has been talk sometimes about changing things, it probably won't happen.

Now I was looking forward to Brad's visit at the end of this month. I knew we were going to have a great time!

SEEING OTHER PARTS OF NAMIBIA

THE TOUR OF BRAD AND NORENE HOGLE

Chapter 15--August 30-September 6, 2009

After Brad, my son, had taken nearly two days to arrive here from the Seattle area with long flights and layover times, flying from Seattle to Paris, waiting there for 11 hours, then on to Johannesburg where he waited for several hours before flying to Windhoek, the capital of Namibia, we finally met at the small Ondangwa Airport a little bit north of where I was living on Sunday morning at 8:30 AM. You can't imagine how excited I was to see someone from the family here in Ondangwa. I had arranged for him to stay in the Steiner Guesthouse in Windhoek on Saturday night after arriving there on Saturday afternoon before taking the 7:00 AM Sunday flight up to Ondangwa, so he was able to sleep in a "normal" way after the two nights sleeping some on the plane from Seattle to Paris and then from there to Johannesburg.

We had a great time on our holiday and everything with the hired driver and car worked out perfectly. This was a bit "pricey" but I'm happy we did it this way because I would not have felt comfortable driving all that way myself since I hadn't driven at all since arriving here and Brad didn't want to drive. The cars drive on the left side of the road and the driving mechanism is on the right side of the car. Some of the roads we would be traveling on were gravel and/or dirt and are in rather remote areas. I had paid all the money in advance and even though this was a very reputable company, I was a bit uneasy because of the way some things happen in Africa; however it all turned out very well.

Our driver, Agies (Agh-hees), a young man probably in his mid-twenties, was very accommodating to our wants and needs plus being a very good driver. He arrived at my house on Saturday afternoon August 29; we discussed the itinerary and he was back on Sunday morning (actually he slept in the SUV somewhere on the school grounds) and we were off to the airport at 7:50 AM on Sunday morning to pick up Brad at 8:30. It only takes about fifteen minutes to get to the airport but you might say that I was overly anxious to get there. Brad walked through the door at 8:30. We drove back through the village so he could see it and then stopped back at the house for a short time so he could see where his Mama was living and to drop off some things he brought me from home. Also, he saw the school, a classroom, the staff room where I did my work and met a few of my fellow teachers who were waiting for the Grade 8 trip to get organized to leave for Swakopmund over on the western coast, where they were going to spend four days.

Then it was off to Etosha National Park about a 2 ½ hour drive south of Ondangwa. This park "is regarded as one of the world's greatest wildlife viewing venues", according to the Lonely Planet travel guide. "Its name, which means 'Great White Place of Dry Water', is taken from the vast greenish-white Etosha Pan. The Pan is an immense, flat, saline desert covering over 5,000 sq km." When I was there in early February with a few friends it was very wet, with all the rain we were having, so it looked quite different this time and we saw many more animals than at that earlier time. We spent two nights, the first night at a lodge inside the park and the next night at another place 12 kilometers outside the park. After entering the park we drove for over an hour getting to our lodging for the night and in doing this we started to see the animals. Animals we saw driving in and later on the game drives in the safari vehicles included elephants, giraffes, zebras, many springbok, impala, gemsbok, one lion lying under a tree, one leopard lying under a tree and one in a tree with his kill which was a springbok, guinea fowl, eland, wildebeest, kudu, hyenas, jackals, ostriches and many birds of which I can't remember the names. Agies was very good at pointing them out when we didn't see them. He had been here several times before while driving other tourists. Also, he knew the whole routine of how to do things and could speak the language although the people in the "tourist business" know English and some other languages; they have to, in dealing with a variety of people. I had booked a night drive and an early morning drive at Halali, although Agies would have done this for us, but I didn't know it at the time having never hired a car with driver before.

Our accommodations were very nice; at Halali the first night we had what amounted to a one bedroom apartment with kitchenette, living room, bath and large bedroom in our separate chalet. Most of the dinners we had featured game meat one or two of the following: kudu, springbok, oryx, zebra, impala, as well as, beef, chicken, seafood and/or pork plus all the other things that go with a meal. At one place there was crocodile. Any of the game meat I had was very good-poor animals. The breakfasts were buffet with an extensive variety of food. We were certainly WELL FED. This afternoon after getting settled in the chalet, we walked to the water hole to see what was going on there. Although it is quite warm in the afternoon there was a breeze which always helps, so it was quite pleasant sitting in the shade and watching for animals. There were two elephants that came to the water and were squirting water on themselves probably to cool off; there were a few springbok, a number of guinea fowl, and lots of small birds swooping in and out over the water. We enjoyed this and it was very relaxing.

The night drive was interesting but it is a "one-time" experience. It was quite cold and too dark to see much, even with the driver's red night-vision light shining around; he used this kind of light so as not to disturb the animals. I should have figured this out on my own that we wouldn't see much due to the darkness. However, we did see two black (or maybe white) rhinos at one of the water holes and some jackals and hyenas who seemed to be fighting over a "kill". We were given a down garment upon entering the truck which I thought was a blanket but Brad figured out that it was a parka before the night ended.

Monday morning we arose bright and early for the 5:30-8:30 AM safari drive which proved to be much more interesting than the previous night drive. The weather was cold but the parka helped a lot since I wore it the correct way. It was on this occasion that we saw a pride of twelve lions lying there in the grass looking over the field probably to see where the next meal was coming from. The driver/guide said it was most unusual to see this many lions gathered in one place. The male of the group stationed himself somewhat apart from the rest of the group but kept watching the others all the time. We watched them for about an hour. On the drive we saw other animals that we had seen the day before but no elephants. The next interesting sight was a leopard up in a tree with his/her "kill" probably a springbok; we watched this for quite a while. When one spots two or three cars stopped on the road, there is something there to see and other vehicles stop.

After this drive we had the buffet breakfast outside on the patio and then went back to the chalet to pack up to be ready to meet Agies at 11:00 AM to go to the next lodge. I couldn't get two successive nights at any lodge here, even though I had booked three months in advance, hence the reason for moving but this actually turned out well because we experienced two different places and the second place was closer to the highway to drive south on Tuesday. We saw more animals on the drive out which took over an hour arriving at Mushara Outpost in early afternoon. I had booked another game ride for this afternoon but on the way asked Brad if he was up for another one but we both agreed that we had probably seen all the animals we were going to see and after having arisen at 4:45 AM that morning thought a relaxing afternoon sounded good. Our accommodation here was described as a luxury tent which means the bathroom is attached-en suite-but it was a solid building made to look like a tent and, indeed, was luxurious for a tent. I took advantage of the shower in every place we stayed since my shower at my home in Ondangwa was the Shower in a Bag.

Later in the afternoon, I took a walk over to the gift shop to ponder over some very unique napkin rings that were at our luncheon table and anything else that "I couldn't live without". I did buy the napkin rings although the cost was more than I thought it would be. When I left there, about 6:00 P.M., it was dark walking down the path but I had brought my flashlight with me. Here it seems that when darkness comes it is almost instantaneous. There were a number of paths with the "luxury tents" and first I went on the wrong path then doubled back. One of the workers was by a little pond apparently watching me; I told him we were in Tent #1 so he told me which direction to go. I couldn't see any numbers on the posts by the walkways up to the tents so finally when I thought I had walked far enough I turned up the path to the front door (which was in the back) but seeing a lady standing there, I knew it wasn't the right one. She tried to open the door to help me but couldn't get it open but we talked through the glass and she told me theirs was #3 so I walked back to the path and came to the last one which was #1.

That night as we were sitting in a circle around an open pit fire having a drink before dinner, we sat next to the couple in Tent #3 and found they were from England. They were so easy and fun to talk with. Jean asked how long we were going to be there and when I told her we were leaving early the next morning, she said, "Oh, what a pity because we could have such a good time together." We had assigned tables on the outdoor patio area for dinner so couldn't sit with them. It was very pleasant with a balmy temperature and a gentle breeze. At the end of the dinner the kitchen and wait crew came out singing and dancing in a Congo line amongst the tables, then went just inside the dining room and sang several songs for us. This made it a festive evening.

Agies told us we should leave at 6:00 A.M. on Tuesday morning in order to get to Swakopmund, our next destination. We were up at 4:45 again to be ready for breakfast at 5:30 AM. We took our bags to the dining room since no one could drive to the chalets; we were the first ones at the table but a few other "early risers" came a little bit later. Agies didn't arrive until 6:30 which isn't bad but I was thinking, "Oh, I wonder if this is one of those 'Africa time' situations." The receptionist tried to call him and I tried my cell phone but there was no reception there. He had stayed somewhere with his brother the night before and I think didn't judge the time properly, but all ended well. We did see a number of baboons in a group by the side of the road shortly after we left the Etosha area. They scurried away into the bush as we passed them. It took about six hours to get to Swakopmund so we were there in early afternoon. We made two stops along the way. This was the usual pattern to stop every 2 or 3 hours on a long drive if there was a decent place to stop. The towns going south after leaving the Etosha area are larger, more attractive and more neatly kept than those up in the Northern part.

We were definitely in the desert for quite a ways before arriving at Swakopmund for one night. Two of my friends had gone there earlier in the week and texted that it was fun but cold and he was correct, cold and windy. It is Namibia's favorite holiday destination along the Atlantic coastline. It is named Swakopmund because the mouth of the Swakop River feeds into the sea along the border of the town. The following is quoting and paraphrasing from the Lonely Planet book. "It is often described as being more German than Germany with its quirky mix of German-Namibian residents and the mix of German tourists, who feel right at home with the town's German appreciation of comfort and hospitality. It has seaside promenades, half-timbered homes and colonial-era buildings but the sea-side holiday towns of the North Sea and Baltic coasts do not have the wind-blown sand and palm trees of Swakopmund. Thanks to the mild temperatures and negligible rainfall, it enjoys a statistically superb climate (25 degrees C in the summer and 15 degrees in the winter) but when the wind blows, the town gets a sand blasting and the cold winter sea fogs create a drizzle and a dreary atmosphere, but this fog rolls inland up to 50 km and provides life-sustaining moisture for desert plants and animals." When we were walking around the town one of the merchants told us that the only time it is warm and pleasant every day is in December, so I don't know when the person who wrote the account was there; it must have been in December.

After checking in at The Secret Garden Guesthouse and asking Agies to come back at 3:30 PM for our visit to the camel farm outside of town, we walked down to the pier and beach which was only a few blocks from the hotel. It **was** cold and windy as my friend James had said, but exhilarating. We walked out to the end of the pier bracing against the wind. There were only a few people out there; we took the obligatory photos and then walked back stopping at the restaurant there to inquire about dinner reservations. The hostess said she had only a few open spaces at the bar in the smoking area left for dinner. I kind of made a face when she said this for which Brad pointed out to me a little bit later that she was just doing her job so we said, "Thank you," and left. Brad wanted to at least wade in the water of the South Atlantic, so he rolled up his pant legs and walked in a little ways; I declined because I don't like to go in cold water. He said it wasn't bad.

After this we walked down a very lovely promenade lined with palm trees toward the lighthouse and a more protected beach area in kind of a cove. The temperature was better here and the breeze was more gentle and warmer. There were a number of people of all ages walking on the beach and sitting at the several outdoor cafes. One of the most popular restaurants called the Lighthouse Pub and Café with a view of the beach and crashing surf was here. We were successful in making a reservation for dinner for 6:30 PM which is a bit before most dine. I did ask the receptionist if we would be able to get a taxi back to the guesthouse after dinner and she said, "No problem," as is the overused buzzword term now. This was several blocks from the hotel which is very walkable and we do like to walk, but we were warned not to be out walking after dark if at all necessary even in this town. In our walk back we passed the street merchants with their wares displayed mostly on blankets or mats on the ground. Brad did want to get some dolls, masks and other Namibian artifacts to take back home for gifts so we stopped at one which did have nice merchandise. When we asked the price they would tell us but quickly add, "We can discuss it and negotiate after you choose what you want to buy", which is the usual spiel in these kinds of situations. Brad bought quite a number of gift items there which he had planned to do somewhere and was anxious to get it done sooner than later and the final prices were reasonable, I thought after a bit of bargaining. He was pleased with his purchases and, <u>of course</u>, I had to buy a few more things. We did have a pleasant walk and for me it was a different world from up in the north.

That afternoon we drove the 12 kilometers out to the camel farm to have a camel ride; this is something Brad wanted to do. I asked Agies if he had even done that; he hadn't so I invited him to come along, as well. The lady in charge, who was German but born in Namibia, was very friendly and dressed us all up in the typical headgear that you see when you see camel riders. It is to keep the dust and wind from getting to your face and eyes. Ours was a gentle ride so we really didn't need the headdress but it was fun wearing it. The guides led us around a circular path in the desert. The three of us were in a little caravan jostling along there and the camels were very gentle. The temperature was very pleasant, unlike in the town, so it was an interesting and enjoyable experience.

After the ride, we had tea, tea made the real English way, and some cakes. I commented on her lovely cacti and succulent garden and mentioned the welwitschia plant that is unique to Namibia which we had studied in Natural Science and the fact that I would like to see one. She said, "I have two of them, a male and a female" so she took us out to the garden to see them. This plant grows in the very dry desert and is a conifer, the only conifer in Namibia. It grows slowly, has only two wide long leathery leaves which can grow up to 2 metres in length and roots which can be up to 3 metres long and lives for many years. It is about six inches high but spreads out very widely. The male and female both have cones; the female is larger than the male. Some plants are up to 2,000 years old but the mid-sized ones are probably 1,000 years old. This last bit is in case you wanted a little science lesson along the way. Its uniqueness really fascinates me, as you might guess. Brad and Agies may have thought I was a bit "dotty" gushing over this plant but they were polite enough not to say anything.

That night we had our dinner at the Lighthouse Pub and Café which was a pleasant experience. I had asked the receptionist at the guesthouse if she would make arrangements for a taxi for us but apparently when Agies came to pick us up to go the camel farm, they must have talked because when we came out of the rooms she said that our driver would take us. Of course, this was part of his duty, but as I stated previously, having never had a driver before, I didn't think to ask him. He took us to the restaurant at 6:00 PM and came back for us at 8:00 which was perfect timing. When we sat down at the table the receptionist told us that our table was double-booked for the evening so I asked her when the next people were coming and she said at 8:00 PM so this worked out perfectly. When we went downstairs and outside after dinner, Agies was there waiting to drive us back to the guesthouse. That night I was cold in the room and bed. I had asked the manager in late afternoon if there was any heat in the room because I had not seen any controls anywhere. His reply was that it never got below 15 degrees (about 60 degrees F) so there was no need of it; it is the wind that makes it cold. There were blankets in the closet I was told. Well, my thought is "cold is cold whatever makes it cold." I slept with the comforter, a blanket and my long silk underwear on which I had put in at the last minute after James had texted that it was cold down there. Then I was fine; Brad said he didn't have any problem with the lack of heat.

On Wednesday morning we drove down to Walvis Bay, 30 kilometers south of Swakopmund. It is the second largest city in Namibia with a population of 60,000, has the best harbor and is the only real port between Luderitz in the south and Luanda, Angola to the north. It was claimed by the English Cape Colony in 1797 but only annexed in 1878 when it was realized the Germans were interested in the harbor. In 1910, Britain relinquished it to the newly formed Union of South Africa. We learned later, when we were on a city tour of Windhoek, that even though the Germans knew it was a better harbor they were not willing to have any contact with the British so they used Swakopmund as their harbor even though there were difficulties getting passengers and supplies from the ship to the shore.

There were a number of residential buildings–homes, apartments and condos built and being built on the beach area all along the way from Swakopmund because it is a very popular holiday destination. Whenever I see this kind of build-up especially in a desert area, anywhere, I always wonder how there will be enough water to support the population. Agies drove down to the beach area where there were hundreds of flamingos standing out in the water off shore. That was exciting for us; I had not seen that number of flamingos when I was on the trip to Kenya. Walvis Bay appeared to me as a typical upscale desert town like I've seen in California and Arizona with different pastel colored stucco homes mainly with the red tile roofs. It was very clean and "organized". While driving through the town we came upon a parade with the uniformed marching band, some walkers, and the Department of Health cars and vans. This was Pharmacists' week. Just as an aside here, I'm surprised when I see mostly white people in a place as there are in Swakopmund and Walvis Bay because in the North there are very few, at least in the area where I was. I felt sometimes like I was a "freak" in the population with my white skin and red hair although I never felt any discrimination. Only the smaller children stared at me constantly but the rest of the people didn't. I smiled at the children and tried to talk to them a little bit, but what I got in return was the stare; once in a while I received a little smile. The children are all so very beautiful.

After leaving Walvis Bay, we were immediately in the desert traveling in a south easterly direction down to the "big sand dune area". There were opportunities to go "sand boarding" in the Swakopmund and Walvis Bay area which some of my younger colleagues did while visiting there. Driving along we passed a variety of landscapes including flat sandy areas bare of vegetation and some with shrubs, areas with green grass and shrubs, rugged mountains, rounded mountains/hills and canyons. There is one place to stop for petrol, refreshment, etc. and it is appropriately named Solitaire. Although it is just a "wide spot in the road" the area does have some guest farms, camping places, and lodges. Agies told us that we could get really good apple pie there and indeed it was very tasty. There is a general store, restaurant, bathrooms, and a bakery with quite a variety of baked goods. The baker was a rather rotund gentleman, probably from South Africa, who was very personable and loved to talk to everyone who came in to the shop. While Brad and I were sitting out in the patio area eating our apple pie, he came over and said he would love to know how to make a lemon meringue pie. Not being a great pie baker myself, I couldn't remember all the ingredients, although I have made a few in the past. I told him that he could look it up on Google. He said he didn't have internet, but someone in the store did so he would have her find it.

We arrived at our destination, Sesriem, about 3:00 PM. Sesriem means six thongs which was the number of joined leather ox-wagon thongs necessary to draw water from the bottom of the nearby gorge. This is where the park headquarters, a small food shop, a gift shop, a petrol station and the Sossusvlei Lodge is. The park entry permits are sold here which we needed to go into the park the next morning at sunrise. We bought a few little items at the gift shop, of course, then we drove back up the road to the Desert Homestead and Horsetrails Lodge for our two nights' accommodations. I had tried to book at the Sossusvlei Lodge back in May but it was all full even at that time, but Horsetrails was very pleasant. Ours was a nice rustic room; all the rooms were in separate cabins. We both did some laundry and had a shower with cold water, but it wasn't too bad. The weather was warm but there was a breeze so it was quite pleasant.

After the "chores" were finished, we went down to the patio outside of the restaurant to have a cold drink while overlooking the swimming pool, the desert and the mountains in the distance. While waiting for dinner a little later, we met several of the staff who were from the Ondangwa or Oshakati area up north who knew where Heroes School was. Some said they would contact me when they were in the area, but I doubted if this would happen since they didn't know my name. They were at this lodge and others because they had gone to food service and/or hotel management school in Windhoek and the jobs were down at these desert lodges. It was to bed fairly early because we had to get up at 4:30 AM the next morning for our "dune experiences."

On Thursday morning it was an early rise to have a light breakfast-tea, juice, cereal and/or bread, pick up the boxed breakfasts and meet Agies at 5:30 AM for the 30 kilometer drive to Sesriem where the gate to Sossusvlei opened at 6:00 AM for those who wanted to see the sun rise over the dunes, which is what most of the people do. After we had traveled a short distance, we were flagged down by a young couple from our lodge, who had a flat tire on their rental 4WD. The man was down by the wheel and his wife did the flagging. They had two spare tires, as everyone who rents (or hires, as they say here) a car is advised to carry, but there was no jack. Agies quickly jumped out of the car to see how he could help, then got the jack out of our car and went to work with the man while the rest of us took pictures of the event. This is the way the labor was divided for this project. He jacked the car up while the young man tended to the wheel. It took probably less than ten minutes for the whole operation. They thanked us profusely for stopping where upon the young woman handed him a six-pack of Windhoek lager when he was finished. When we were back in the car he said, "I have a beer." That night at dinner I told him I was impressed with the quick way he helped that couple. He replied that he liked to do what was needed and when you are out in the lonely desert, people do have to help each other. The AAA or the rental cars' offices are pretty far away.

Meanwhile, to get back to the story, we did arrive at the gate a little after 6:00 AM and drove the 45 kilometers to the very popular and "climbable" Dune 45, so named because it is that far from Sesriem, stopping a few times to watch and photograph the sun rising over the dunes of which there are many. The landscape is constantly changing with the wind forever altering the shape of the dunes and the colors shifting with the changing light. This dune is 150 meters high but some are as high as 300 meters. There were already people at the top of the dunes when we arrived there. Those staying at Sesriem can enter the park at 5:00 AM. Agies waited for us at the parking area while Brad and I started the climb. It wasn't that difficult but walking/slogging through the sand took a bit of extra energy. I did have my hiking pole with me and I think this helped. I stopped one of the people coming down and asked if she would take a photo of the two of us-mother and son-which she did. Brad decided that he wanted to go back down at one point, but I elected to go to the top of the first dune; I think I got a "second wind" because it didn't seem as strenuous as the first part. My feeling was that I had heard so much about Dune 45 and had come quite a distance so I was determined to climb it.

Next we drove to a pickup point where the park people drive the visitors in safari vehicles to the next point of interest 5 kilometers away. Agies knew this whole routine and was our guide for the rest of the experience. He knew which vehicles were the park's and which belonged with the private tours. This is where "Big Daddy", the largest dune, is. We walked out towards it to a very dry cracked earth salt pan in front of it, where there were dead camel thorn trees that are being held up by very long roots. Their trunks and branches were dead white. There was one place where there were green trees. No one was climbing Big Daddy, probably because it was becoming hotter at this time. There was still a gentle breeze all the time we were in the dunes and this helped greatly. Then we boarded another safari vehicle to visit another area of dunes and some vegetation on the lower part. In the parking area of each of these places there were several large shade trees with picnic tables and benches. At this place there appeared an oryx on one of the hills. He had stopped and was looking all around. This was kind of exciting to see; it reminded me somewhat of some commercial for an insurance company, I think, (of which I cannot recall) where there is a "deer type" animal on a mountain surveying the scene, maybe it is Hartford. Agies walked with us on the flat area to a point and then I thought I would like to walk up on the hill where there were green trees and shrubs to go back to the parking area. After this we were taken back to the main pick-up point to go back to Sesriem. It really felt good to me to have done that much walking. It was definitely warmer now but some people were just starting the tours; I was happy that we had begun ours earlier in the morning.

As we were heading back to Sesriem I asked Agies to stop at Park Headquarters there because I wanted to peruse the store once more. I wanted to get a "coffee table type" book about Namibia but it was $320 and I knew it was less at The Book Den in Windhoek which we would visit later. I bought a few postcards, then we stopped at the petrol station. I thought our tour was finished at that point but Agies said we had one more stop which was at the nearby Sesriem Canyon. It is about one kilometer long and thirty meters deep. It was quite impressive even though it wasn't Fish River Canyon in the south or the "granddaddy" of all canyons, The Grand Canyon in Arizona. We walked around for awhile at the top and saw people way down at the bottom; Brad and I decided we didn't particularly want to go to the bottom and when we joined Agies again, he said we would take a little walk. Guess where we went?-to the bottom of the canyon where there is a brackish pool of water covered with green moss at the head of the canyon. I was glad that we did do that walk, however; it wasn't difficult but one, especially one who had a broken knee before, just had to be very careful. Agies stated that there is water in the bottom of the canyon during the rainy season up to about a meter high.

After this we headed back to the lodge arriving in early afternoon. Both of us felt we had put in a full day already of nine hours so we welcomed the afternoon time to relax. We had lunch outside on the restaurant patio then reorganized, showered, repacked and rested until dinner time. I wrote a few postcards to family members. The postcards at our lodge were $6.50 to $8.00, instead of the usual $3, so I only bought a few but realized later that I was "nickel and diming" some things because after spending a few thousand dollars U.S. for the trip it didn't make a whole lot of sense not wanting to pay 50 cents more for a postcard. We invited Agies to join us for dinner this night since it would be our last night together. I don't know how much he enjoyed it but we did get to know him a little bit better and we enjoyed having him with us. He liked the meal, I'm sure. The four-course dinner menu, for the two nights we were here, didn't include any game meat; one night was roast pork and the other was beef. The meals were very good and quite filling. Everyone was served the same thing; I usually gave part of my dinner to Brad rather than sending it back uneaten. I felt this had been a very good day once again, and we had seen everything we had planned.

Friday morning's rising time was 6:00 AM (not quite as early as yesterday) for breakfast and then the drive back to Windhoek. Agies arrived at 7:15 AM and we were on the road again at 7:30. Our first stop was at Solitaire again where Agies had apple pie, Brad had a meat pie and I had a jam tart. We talked to the baker again and he said he was going to get the recipe for the lemon meringue pie that day. From here Agies took a northeasterly direction on a D road which is a District road mainly of dirt and some gravel but manageable in a regular car. Once again we were able to see a different kind of landscape of hills and mountains mostly. We crossed a few mountain passes, the highest of which was Spreetshoogte 2005 meters high, not the pass but the mountain. We did pass an occasional home on this route. At the top of the pass was a larger building with a parking lot which seemed a little strange to me. Upon asking, Agies said that it was a meeting place for the farmers of the area.

The drive back only took four and a half hours so we were in Windhoek before noontime. What a difference this city was from where we had been! Agies delivered us to the Steiner Guesthouse and we said our good-byes. I gave him the rest of the snacks and fruit we hadn't eaten and a generous gratuity, I hope, and a hug. We wished him good luck on the rest of his trips and said we would e-mail some pictures to him which we did. We were in rooms 7 and 9 upstairs which are nicer and larger than the ones downstairs where I had stayed before. At Etosha and Desert Homestead we shared a room with twin beds because accommodations were so tightly booked and it worked out well. After getting settled, we walked to the big Namibian Craft Centre which was only a few blocks away. Brad had expressed interest in this; I had been there in May but didn't buy anything at that time knowing I would be back in September. It has everything there that anyone can think of at reasonable prices. Items do have a set price and there is no bargaining. He bought some more things for gifts for now and Christmas and I bought some things to take home for my "Africa Experience" to share and keep for myself.

We were back at the guesthouse by 3:00 PM to relax, look at our purchases, etc. About an hour or so later we walked over to the KFC across the way to get something for dinner. This eating establishment is very popular here in Namibia. My learners often said their favorite food is KFC. There are no McDonalds here or other fast food places popular in America that I know of except Wimpy's; I don't know if this is a branch of the ones in the States or maybe it comes from England. Whenever I'd gone to the KFC, which is only a few times, there have been long lines of customers waiting to order or pick up food. The Steiner serves breakfast and lunch but no dinner so KFC comes in handy for a casual dinner. We sat out in the patio area by the swimming pool for about two hours eating and talking this evening. This little tropical courtyard setting of the patio was very pleasant and relaxing. The hotel has done a nice job with the planting of trees and plants. One is not aware of the busy city outside of the gates and walls. It was dark at 6:00 PM and we were up in our rooms about 7:00 PM for the night.

Our plan for Saturday was to walk along Independence Avenue, the main street of Windhoek, which I thought Brad should see, but also there were a few things that I wanted to get, look around, go to the big mall and then go back to the guesthouse to await the City Tour which I had booked at Brad's suggestion for the afternoon. The Steiner is about a 10-minute walk to Independence Avenue; this is one reason I liked to stay there, plus the price is right and it is an attractive place. We asked at the Book Den, where I did purchase two big books about Namibia, for the location of a fabric store, because I wanted to buy "an Africa type" material to make a tablecloth and napkins when I got back home. The lady gave directions to the store. On the way back from there we saw and purchased some 2010 calendars with African scenes.

Shortly after 2:00 P.M. Adolph arrived with the Gourmet Tours van to pick us up for the city tour of Windhoek. He informed us very quickly that there are good people named Adolph making reference to "you know who." There were already two passengers on board, a mother and daughter from Mali. The daughter was probably 40-45 years old and spoke very good English. She had gone to university in France and had spent several years in America. Mama spoke no English so the daughter translated for her what was said. Then we went to a residential area up in one of the suburbs to pick up the other three people for the tour. Adolph had a little trouble in finding their home but finally did arrive at the correct place. These were a mother, her teenage daughter and a young adult son. They had lived in Windhoek for a number of years, also in Germany, but had never really seen the city as so often happens. Brad got to sit up in front with Adolph in the passenger seat. As you may know, Windhoek exhibits a strong German influence. Namibia became a protectorate of Germany in the 1880's and was known as German South West Africa. Adolph explained things mostly in English but did speak some German or perhaps it was Afrikaans to mother and children. First we went up into the high part of the city to Schwerinsburg Castle and Water Tower-Hill so we could see the whole expanse of the city. There was somewhat of a haze over the entire city although the day was bright and sunny.

Windhoek's best-recognized landmark is the German Lutheran

Church (Christuskirche), a beautiful church on a traffic island up near the Government Gardens. We went into the church for a brief time. It is very beautiful with stained glass windows, rich-looking wood and the other appointments that most churches of that era contain. I asked if it was for the Namibians or just for Germans and was told just the latter go there. The cornerstone was laid in 1907. Directly across from the church are the Government Gardens and the Ink Palace, so called because a lot of ink was used (wasted) on government documents especially before Independence. I wouldn't be surprised if the same thing is going on now from what I read in the newspapers. The gardens are very lovely; while we were viewing them there were two weddings being held there with the two processions walking in from separate sides and gathering in a separate area. It is a beautiful setting for any kind of formal event or just a place to sit, relax and meditate.

The next place of interest was the old Cape-Dutch-style Train Station and Trans-Namib Transport Museum. Across from the entrance is the German Steam Locomotive, *Poor Old Joe,* which was shipped to Swakopmund in 1899, and then reassembled for the run to Windhoek. We didn't go upstairs to see the museum because it was getting late and there was still another place to go. The guard was very busy sitting and watching the soccer match on TV between Namibia and Swaziland, which Swaziland won, we heard later.

The final destination of the afternoon tour was a drive through the Katutura area of the city. This is the very poor area. Adolph said there are 1800 bars here and we saw many, one right after the other much like the ones up in Ondangwa. They were small and had interesting names. There were many people out at this time, perhaps because it was after 5:00 PM on a Saturday night. They waved to us as we went by. A number of people were fixing their evening meal on the outdoor *braais* (barbeques) so there was quite a bit of smoke in the air. Actually in looking over the city earlier, I commented about the haze wondering if there were forest fires and Adolph said it came from veldt fires from Botswana, Namibia and South Africa. People aren't supposed to be burning rubbish and other things but they do it anyway.

There were lots of shack-type buildings and many rectangular flat-roofed metal structures each housing a family of several people. Regarding the metal buildings, Adolph termed it as a "Mafia-type" operation in which businesses buy the buildings, set them up, and then charge outrageous prices for people to rent them. The population of Windhoek is 240,000 and 2/3 of the people, 160,000, live in Katutura. Before getting to a better part of this area, we passed a very large cemetery with rather crude grave markers where AIDS victims were buried. It really was stark-looking as a reminder of this terrible disease which affects from 21% to 29% of the population in this country. There is a better-looking part of Katutura with stucco homes and there seems to be a government program in force to get better housing to more people. Quoting from the Lonely Planet book, "Unlike its South African counterparts, the township of Katutura is relatively safe by day if you stick to the northern areas or find someone who can act as a guide." It was an interesting tour so I'm glad Brad suggested it. I had sent him several pieces of information and maps for him to peruse that I had gathered up in May when I was in Windhoek.

Shortly after 6:00 PM we were delivered back to the Steiner. The two Mali ladies were let off first. The mother was quite large but beautifully dressed in a native type costume with the matching headgear scarf but the daughter wore Western attire. When we were at Christ Church, we took photos of the two of them and then Brad asked if he might have his picture taken with the mother. Her daughter asked her and she apparently said, "No she didn't wish to have her picture taken with anyone else", so he thanked them and said he understood. The mother was attending a convention at this really fancy hotel which I thought must be very expensive but when I looked it up in the book later, I thought the price was reasonable for such an upscale place.

Dinner this Saturday night was at the very popular Joe's Beer House where I had been with the group in May. When I first heard the name I thought it must be some kind of a "dive" but it isn't. It is a touristy spot but has an African motif throughout so I thought we must go there on this trip. All kinds of game meat are served, plus a few other regular meats and they have one or two vegetarian entrees. I had made reservations several weeks before. We were seated with two young ladies which was a surprise to me because I thought we would have a table to ourselves but it turned out very well. At first we were what I would say "socially polite" but once we started talking it was a lot of fun getting to know something about them. They had just arrived from Switzerland that morning and were going on a four-week holiday throughout Namibia in a rental car with rented camping gear. Brad told them to be sure they had a jack. The only reservations they had made were at Sesriem where the popular dunes are. They were just going to go where their trip would take them. This sounds like kind of a nice way to take a trip if you have plenty of time. They work at Telecom in Switzerland

and did have names of contacts from this company here in Namibia whom they were going to contact. I bought my internet device from Telecom. We each ordered a combination dinner which was very good. I think it had oryx, kudu and something else. Brad probably remembers exactly but sometimes I get my dinners and events mixed up in my mind as to where or when something happened from being in a number of different places at different times. I do know that oryx was the most tender of anything I've had--poor oryx. The only disappointment of the evening was that the gift shop was closed when we finished dinner; Brad had wanted a tee shirt from there which I said I would buy him for his birthday but I did get it later in December when I was back there

We met for breakfast at 7:30 AM on Sunday morning in order to have time for last minute packing and tidying up. The breakfast is buffet style with many items from which to choose-cereals, juice, bread, cheeses, cold cuts, fruit, other pastries, jams, jellies, boiled eggs, plus one can have a cooked breakfast, as well, as is the custom in many countries except in the U.S. We ate out on the enclosed sun porch. Brad was able to take some of my "gift things" in his bag. He had given away almost all of his clothes, as planned, to the housekeeper who came into his room that morning to clean, so he had room for the things he had purchased. His transport arrived at 9:30 AM to take him to the big airport for his 12:00 something flight to Johannesburg, so we said our good-byes. I surely hated to see him go but was so happy that he was able to make the trip over to this "little-known" country which we know a lot more about now.

After he left I finished up a few things and then checked out and stored my bags in the hotel's storage room because I wasn't leaving for the small airport until about 1:00 PM for my flight to Ondangwa. I took one more trip down Independence Avenue and to the mall where I spent some time at the internet café, then had a fruit salad with soft ice cream before walking back. You can see where my "thrills" came from. Yvonne, at the desk, arranged for me to go to the airport early because the time had changed in Namibia early Sunday morning moving ahead one hour and she did trust South African Air to go at the correct time internationally which Brad had taken, but didn't know about the local flights. I had about a two hour wait at Eros Airport for the 3:00 PM flight but it was comfortable and I had time to read the newspaper and part of a book I was working through. The flight was full; there are only 21 seats on these small planes and it is comfortable.

Upon arriving at the Ondangwa Airport at 4:30 PM, the plane stopped quite a distance from the gate so we had to walk about the equivalent of three blocks to the terminal. One lady walking beside me explained that the plane didn't have enough fuel to take us up to the gate, then go back to the fuel pump to fill up again. This was a first to my ears. I was hoping to find a taxi to take me home but there were none in sight. I had been to this airport a few times and there were always a few taxis there but seeing none I started walking out to the road where I would be able to flag one down eventually. I had my backpack, a wheeled backpack and a plastic zipped carrying bag which a lot of people here use as their luggage, filled with all my purchases mostly, plus my purse so I was heavily laden, but I thought, "I can do this!" I had only gone a short distance when a young man (probably about 40 years old-young to me) flagged me down and asked if I would like a ride. He had been on the plane and said he heard me say when I was going into the terminal that I hoped I could find a taxi. He had booked a rental car at the airport. He was from Windhoek and was going up to Oshakati on business for two days. I told him I was going south so it would be out of his way. I was happy to hear him say it was no problem, so he brought me right up to my doorstep and helped carry the bags inside. We talked on the way; he said he goes up to this area about once a month and usually drives which takes about 8 hours, is here for two days and then has the long drive back on Tuesday afternoon arriving back there in the middle of the night so just decided to spend the extra money and have a relaxing trip.

I was happy to be back in Ondangwa and grateful that everything turned out the way it was planned. I always felt fortunate that I was able to see and do a variety of things in Namibia. Now it was back to getting ready for Term 3 of the school year.

BRAD HOGLE'S ACCOUNT OF OUR NAMIBIAN HOLIDAY

Chapter 16--August 27-September 7, 2009

Here is the copy, just the way he wrote it:
Subject: Namibia
I recently returned from a visit to the southern African country of Namibia to visit my mom. For those of you who don't know, she is volunteer teaching in the northern part of that country near the Angolan border until this December, having arrived there in January, through an organization out of Harvard University called World Teach. When she first told me last May she was going to embark on this excursion, I first asked her where the country was, as I had never heard of it (it borders South Africa to the northwest), and it still took me about three days to remember the name and spelling of it. In the same conversation, she said that she hoped I would come visit while she was there, and of course I knew that was an unexpected and most likely once-in-a-lifetime opportunity and I certainly did hope to take advantage of that chance. My journey from here to there and back lasted August 27-September 7. Since Mom had two major holidays during the school year and I couldn't make it for the first one in spring, then it was definite that I would be going to visit during the time period that I did and I was able to start planning and researching things six months early. My flight arrangements were made in mid-February and due to this, I was able to use frequent-flyer miles for the majority of the trip (it's nice to know that those programs can actually work). During Mom's

first break, she made most of the arrangements. I had a couple ideas of what I wanted to see while I was there after reading up on the country and discovering such a diverse landscape, but I left everything in her hands, as I knew she would do a great job in planning things and I wouldn't have known where to start, and as it turned out, this was the case. So here goes the chronological recap of things.

Thursday, August 27-Saturday, August 29 (Travel time)
I boarded Air France out of Sea-Tac in the early afternoon in preparation for the long journey, which would involve four additional cities or towns and three different airlines before finally arriving in mom's area. The first leg was to Paris, where I arrived early in the morning their time. For some reason I was unable to sleep at all during the long journey, and that caused me to alter my first plans, which had been to take the subway from the airport into central Paris and try and visit some landmarks since I had an eleven-hour layover. But due to the lack of sleep, I was so out of it when arriving at Charles de Gaulle Airport there and I just didn't feel up to traveling around, plus I couldn't find any indication of how to even get to the subway station. At that time sleep sounded really good and I knew that Paris would always be there, so I decided to just hang out at the airport. The eleven hours went pretty fast actually and it was fine, as it wasn't very busy at all, so I almost felt like I had free reign of the place. I did a lot of walking around, scouted out all the shops and what I would possibly want to buy on my way back, used the internet there, did crosswords, read and best of all, I was able to lay out and get a couple hours of sleep which really refreshed me. I used my backpack as my pillow and tied the straps around my fingers so no one would be able to yank it while I was asleep and had the passport in my money belt, so I felt fine regarding getting to sleep. I ate a couple times there also, even though the food was pretty expensive. It's a pretty nice airport, as it has a wide and open feel and you don't really feel cramped at all in there. Eventually that evening it was time to board the next flight, the last of the Air France ones, to Johannesburg, South Africa. This flight was only half-full, so I was able to stretch across the whole row and sleep several hours. We arrived at J'burg Tambo Airport early Saturday morning, and this is where I had my only "interesting" encounter regarding customs. The non-South Africans had their own line to wait in to first show their passport, and when one would get to the front of it, their picture would be taken with some sort of infra-red camera. When it was my turn, I was asked to remove my glasses and after my picture was

taken, the customs agent calls me over and says "Your head is too warm." I just kind've said "Huh? I don't understand", which was the truth, because I had absolutely no idea what was going on. So he says again "Your head is too warm.", and I asked him what that meant, that I wasn't sick and felt fine. Next thing I knew I was being escorted to a nearby nurse's office, where some nice lady had me fill out some vital information and then she took my temperature (they put the thermometer under your armpit there). The reading turned out to be normal, so I was then escorted back to the original customs agent who let me go through. So that was definitely an unexpected experience! Perhaps they're worried about viruses or diseases coming into the country so they take that extra precaution. I had another long layover, about eight hours this time, so did pretty much the same thing as in Paris, although I didn't sleep here since I didn't feel like I needed to. It was interesting noticing how much cheaper things were here in J'burg as opposed to Paris, probably at least 1/3rd the price of something comparable and I'd read that J'burg was one of the cheapest cities in the world and even for airport prices things were reasonable. Kind've a funny comparison is that if you bought a bottle of beer, it was 13 S.A. Rand while a bottle of water was 14! (The current conversion rate is about 7.5 Rand per U.S. dollar-when Mom arrived in January, it was nearly 10 Rand). In early afternoon, it was time to transfer on to South African Airways for the two hour flight to Windhoek, the Namibian capital and largest city, population 220,000. SAA really was quite the luxurious airline, a throwback to how the U.S. airlines used to be. Even though it was only a two-hour flight, we were served a full lunch, two drinks and they used actual silverware and real plates. Touchdown at Windhoek's Hosea Kutako International Airport was a little rough but we made it on the ground fine. The airport is pretty small for an international airport and is only 40 years old. Once I cleared customs and picked up my bags, I saw the shuttle driver that the hotel I'd be staying in that night had sent to pick me up holding a sign with my name, so I was glad that came off without a hitch, as the airport is 26 miles outside of the city and I didn't want to have to rely on a taxi driver who might rip me off regarding the fare. There were three other people in the shuttle with me, including one of only three Americans I saw my entire time there, some young guy from Atlanta. The ride took about 1/2 hour to get into Windhoek, so I enjoyed my first look at the Namibian desert and countryside, including a family of baboons hanging on a fence next to the road. There is absolutely no civilization between the airport and the city, but the airport had to be built that far out due to the fact that there wasn't enough flat land for an airstrip any closer (the elevation of Windhoek is about 5,500 feet/1,680 meters). I was dropped off at my hotel, the Hotel Steiner Pension (I think 'pension' is the word they use in place of 'hotel', as I saw countless 'pensions' around town) about 3:00 PM. I stayed at the hotel the rest of the day, other than walking across the street to get some KFC for dinner. I'm not a huge fast-food fan at all, but it was convenient, so I brought my three pieces of chicken and twelve napkins to absorb the grease back to the hotel and ate it there outside in the courtyard. One note about KFC--that was the ONLY American fast-food outlet I saw in Namibia and even those were very sporadic. It's kind've nice that McDonald's and Starbucks are not in the country. The only other clue of a chain that I saw while on the trip was an English hamburger place called Wimpy's. I stayed outside until about 6:30 and went to the room then, as it was already dark (this time of year, the sun rises about 6 and sets at 6). The temperature was very pleasant and the nice thing about the country is that even if it's hot in the daytime, it does cool down at night, down into the low-50sF for the most part. I soon went to bed, as I would have to get up early the next morning. Boy did that bed look good to me, after the two days of pretty much nothing but airplanes and airports!

Sunday, August 30
I was picked up at the hotel at 6:00 AM by Efrain, the same shuttle driver as the day before, to be taken to Windhoek's other (and original) airport-Eros, for my 7:00 flight on Air Namibia to Ondangwa. An hour was PLENTY of time to allow between getting to the airport and the flight, as Eros is a very, very tiny airport-you could walk the whole thing in about 20 seconds. Eros is in town and is primarily used now for intra-country flights, and on this day there were only two the whole day. The plane was a 2-prop, 17-seater (one seat on each side of the aisle with one row of three seats in the back), with about 10 on board for this flight. No bathroom and no flight attendants-the gate agent handed us our breakfast, earplugs, facial wipe and barf bag as we were walking out of the terminal-it was all in one handy-dandy cellophane wrapped container. Even on this dinky airplane, the food was still way more substantial than what you'd get from a U.S. airline. The flight took 1-1/2 hours and we touched down at an even SMALLER airport in Ondangwa! Mom was there to meet me as well as the driver she had hired for six days, a nice gentleman probably in his mid-20s who went by Agies (pronounced something like "Agh-HEES"), although he said his real name was Gottleib Jagger. We stopped at Mom's school

and place of residence (they're together), Heroes Private School, about ten minutes from the airport. It was Sunday and the school was on holiday, but there were still three or four teachers around, so I was introduced to them, and I could tell that they all really loved my mom. I got a tour of her classroom and the faculty lounge, and then we stopped at her apartment for about a half-hour, as I wanted to see it, plus I had brought her some stuff from the U.S. that she wanted to drop off there before we were on our way. And soon we were, on our way to Etosha National Park two hours away, where we'd spend two days at the Halali Lodge. The drive was interesting, I just basically watched everything around me since it was all new, although it did remind me of Mexico. This area is the poorer area of the country, and we saw a lot of people walking everywhere and many donkeys, which is a primary use of transportation for those who don't have cars, which is many. As we turned off the main road which was paved (about 12% of the country's roads are paved) onto the direction of Etosha, the road turned to gravel (but not too bad condition and very wide). As it turned out, the majority of the roads we'd travel would be gravel. It's mainly our equivalent of what we'd call "interstates" that are paved, one lane each direction, and that's really all that is needed. When we'd come to the occasional town, they'd usually turn into two lanes each direction until we were out of the town again. The paved roads were in very good condition, comparable (or maybe even better) than ours here in the U.S. On the way to Etosha I saw my first African animal, the springbok. Springboks are the most common animal by far, and according to Agies, the zebra comes in second. I can't remember for sure, but I believe we were in the park boundaries at the time I got to see my first "real" African animal--a group of elephants grazing pretty close to the road. A good indication that there might be an animal ahead is if you see another car pulled over to the side of the road. There were signs posted all over with the obvious "Stay In Your Car", but as we approached the elephants, which were very close to the road, a group of Japanese tourists jumped out of their van in order to take pictures of them. Fortunately for them the elephants didn't seem irritated by it, but definitely not a smart thing for them to do--we're not at a zoo!! Before we got to the lodge we got to see a lot more animals, some of them by the side of the road and others at watering holes, as Agies knew where all the watering holes were-Mom and I wouldn't have had a clue. At the first watering hole I got my initial view of zebras, oryx and kudu. A little further down we were lucky to see a lion no more than fifty feet away from us laying under a tree. There were kudu also in the area keeping their distance from her but all of them knew that they were all around, and a couple of the kudus kept making sounds, possibly warning signs to others. The lion seemed pretty content just to rest-she got up once and the animals scattered, but then she laid right back down. And further down the road we got to see a rare sight-a leopard. He/she was just laying around under a tree also. We soon arrived at the lodge and settled in for the afternoon. There is a watering hole at the lodge, so in the afternoon we walked over to it. We saw mainly springbok drinking from there, and then they all scattered but we didn't know why at first. About five minutes later, a male elephant showed up, and a few minutes after that, a female one, and they spent about a half-hour there so we got a great show. Then they took off and when we looked in the distance several minutes later, we saw apparently the rest of the family-about six of them. For dinner that evening I tried kudu, which was delicious (tasted like chicken fried steak) and also crocodile (which I would compare to pork chops). After dinner from 7-10 PM (it was dark by 7:00) we went on a night safari. It was chilly in the jeep, but they provided parka blankets, which we needed. The driver didn't use headlights but used a red searchlight instead, as he said it was better on the animals' eyes and didn't tend to scare them off as much. He really had a good sense of where an animal might be, I don't think any of us in the jeep would ever have spotted anything without him. We did get to see a pair of rare white rhinoceroses at a watering hole apparently having some sort of a tussle, but it wasn't that clear, as it was in the distance and the red light pretty much only provided a "shadow" look at them. It was the same thing for a pack of jackals trying to wrestle away some sort of kill from a lone hyena. Seems like it would be an unfair fight, but a hyena can eat through bone so it definitely held its own.

Monday, August 31

We were up early this morning for a 5:30 AM safari before we checked out of this Lodge. This turned out to be the best safari one could have hoped for, as we found a pride of about twelve lions very close to the road at a watering hole, the closest one only about 40 feet away from us. So we stayed there for at least thirty minutes just watching them do their thing (or not do their thing). There wasn't too much movement, as the guide seemed to think that they had just finished an ample meal. Most of them were very close together, but there was one male all by himself probably at least 150 feet away from the others. After saying goodbye to the lions we continued back towards the lodge and saw a couple cars and buses pulled over in the distance, the obvious clue that there was something to see. What we saw was a leopard up a tree with its kill, a poor springbok. So we got to see two leopards in two days. We returned to the Lodge and had breakfast and then checked out and headed to our next destination, the Mushara Lodge, not too far away and just outside the Etosha park limits. We had planned to go on another safari that afternoon but decided instead just to rest and forget about it, as we felt we had already hit the jackpot and wouldn't see anything new that we hadn't seen and definitely nothing to top the pride of lions and the leopard. So we took it easy for a few hours, enjoying the quiet, until dinnertime. For dinner I had eland. Not an especially attractive animal, but boy did it taste good-had a teriyaki flavor to it. One of the vegetables they had was red beets, which I used to hate as a kid and nothing has since changed. But like a good boy, I finished my plate without holding my nose, although I wanted to. The staff at the Lodge, after dinner was finished, provided entertainment, singing for about twenty minutes, most of them sounded like hymns.

Tuesday, September 1

This was the day to head to the coast, our destination being the German town of Swakopmund, the third-largest town in the country, population 29,000. And this would be the only day of the trip where we'd experience chilly weather (other than the nighttime safari ride). We left the lodge and were on our way for the six-hour drive. The road was paved all the way and was again in very good condition. We had about four or five towns to go through on the way, and we stopped at four of them for "rest stops"-Tsumeb (where we saw a family of baboons hanging out by the road just outside of town), Otjiwarongo, Karibib and Usakos before eventually getting to Swakopmund. Agics had the radio on to one of the few stations that could be received, so we heard some Namibian music. It was interesting, as the primary beat-keeper seems to be the snare drum, and it sounded like Irish and Mexican influences with accordion seeming to be prominent. It was a little eerie to see the fog hugging the coast as we approached Swakopmund, just for the reason that I hadn't seen a single cloud the whole trip up to this point. We arrived in town early afternoon and decided that in a couple hours we'd drive outside of town to a camel farm, as although camels aren't in Namibia as far as I know, I did read about this camel farm and still thought it would be fun and unique to ride one and probably the closest I'd ever get to do so. But before that, we walked down to the beach, which was only a couple blocks away from our hotel, as I wanted to say that I had dipped my toes in the African Atlantic Ocean. There is a pier there and we walked out on it before walking onto the sand. The sand was primarily an off-white color with a touch of purple. We then walked along the promenade to another area of the beach where we saw merchants with their wooden artifacts laid out, so I stopped to browse there, as that was definitely something I had planned to bring back home with me. So, after choosing several things, I was ready to "negotiate" since nothing had a price on it intentionally. I'm not good at that type of thing as it bothers me to do that since I know that I have it better than they do, so in order to avoid any guilt and since the person was very nice, I "played the game" once and bid below what they were asking and then let them come back a little higher before I accepted. I'm sure I could've done better but I was happy with what I was paying and I then walked away with a clear conscience. However, it was a different story about fifteen minutes later when I really was hustled. I had stepped onto the grass to take a picture of a beautiful building, and suddenly a guy appeared and said 'hello' and asked my name. Well silly me, I thought he was just being polite and greeting me, so when he found out my name, his buddy suddenly appeared and started carving my name into some sort of decorative nut. And then I was dumb enough (probably still shell-shocked) to give them Mom's name next, and hers was soon being carved into another one. When it was all said and done, they wanted $200 Namibian dollars each for each nut, and Mom told them "I can buy that for $40!!", and of course they were saying how this was "personally endorsed" and how now they couldn't sell it to anyone else (which wasn't true-they could've easily scratched out our names and tried to sell it to the next sucker besides myself). Since they weren't that nice, I told them I wasn't paying $200 for each one, and since a little part of me did want the thing and wanted to get rid of them, I did eventually talk them down and settled on $200 total for both of them. And as I was pulling out my money, they said "Yes, we have a deal-$300 for both" and Mom said "That's $200!!". I think she's been through this type of thing before but I bit, and after that I didn't and therefore didn't stop on any corners to take any pictures, just in case!! We then walked back to the hotel and Agies soon was there to take us out to the camel farm about ten minutes outside of town, where we had a very relaxing couple of hours. It was run by a very nice lady and Agies joined us on the ride. Mom's camel was Elsa, Agies' was Kalahari, and mine was either Idi or Edie. It didn't occur to me until we had already left that it could've been a male or a female, as when the lady told us its name was Idi, for some reason I only thought of Idi Amin, although I did kind've wonder why she'd want to name a camel after him. The camels were all tied together and we were led around by a couple of the co-workers. It was a little bumpy but fine. The most adventurous part was when the camel would get up at the beginning of the ride or drop down at the end, that's when you needed to be holding on with two hands, since it was a quick jerk and the camel didn't really care if you were prepared or not. After the ride the lady made tea for us and the four of us had a nice chat for about a half-hour and then she wanted to show us her garden which she took a lot of pride in. We then returned back to town and had a nice dinner of oryx steak that evening at a restaurant that overlooked the beach. It was very chilly that evening, as the wind was blowing pretty good. The high was probably in the 60sF for the day and I was reminded of San Francisco and the Bay Area, as like S.F., Swakopmund would be chilly, but once you got just a few miles out, it was quite warm.

Wednesday, September 2
We left Swakopmund for our six-hour drive to the dune area of Sossusvlei. We would only pass two signs of civilization the entire way. The first one being the seaport town of Walvis Bay, the second most populous town (population 60,000) in the country and Namibia's only deep water port and just about ten minutes down the coast from Swakopmund and home to thousands and thousands of flamingos. I'd wondered why the nation's second and third most populous towns were so close to each other, and I learned that Walvis Bay was settled by the English and Swakopmund by the Germans, and the Germans were not about to use Walvis Bay as a port, so they settled in Swakopmund instead. But as it turned out, Swakopmund was a lousy place for a port and the evidence is clear today, as you see no ships there while the typical deep water ships and freighters are visible in Walvis Bay. As soon as we left Walvis Bay, the road quickly went from paved to gravel, but still not in bad condition. The sand soon disappeared and the rest of the trip was through mostly flat desert with a couple small mountain passes, but by no means boring scenery. Cars were few and far between and it took us about twenty-five minutes before we saw our first one. You have a clue usually at least a minute beforehand that a car is coming when you look ahead and see a dust cloud. After nearly five hours we arrived at the other establishment besides Walvis Bay, an oasis out in the middle of nowhere appropriately named Solitaire, which consisted of a convenience store, bakery, restaurant, small motel, and the most important

item-a gas station. It's important when driving the country to have a good map, such as one from the Automobile Association that has the "gas pump" symbol on it, as if you don't, you could really be in a lot of trouble. Business is good in Solitaire as you would expect, and I think EVERYONE stops there. I was curious as to how expensive gas might be way out there, but actually it was very reasonable all things considered-about $3.15 per gallon U.S. After our little rest stop we continued on, stopping to pick up our pass for the following morning to enter the dunes area and then to our lodge for the next two nights, the Desert Homestead And Horsetrails. This was a nice setting, bungalows out in the open, with the vast Namibian desert landscape as our view out of the room. Dinner that night was delicious, the main course was regular beef steak, although once again the side dish was the dreaded beets. But I made a fair trade with Mom--some of her steak for all of my beets. We then retired for the evening, as we'd be up early the next morning.

Thursday, September 3
We were up by 5 AM in order to have breakfast and get to the gates when they opened at 6. We got to the gates just a couple minutes late (but it didn't affect anything), as on the way we pulled over to help a young couple who was also staying at the Homestead as they were stranded with a flat tire (which definitely will happen out there with so many gravel, unpaved roads). Their rental car had two spare tires but no jack (moral of the story-if you ever get to Namibia and rent a car, be sure it has a jack!). Agies had a jack and had it fixed for them in about five minutes at most and we were on our way . We soon were amongst the big dunes, some of the largest in the world. And we're not talking about just a few dunes, but mountain ranges worth. It was nice to be there at sunrise and see the sand changing colors. We soon came up to Dune 45, a popular dune to climb. It would probably take about twenty-five minutes to climb, and it's a lot harder than it looks. Walking in soft sand is hard enough, so just imagine trying to do it up a nearly 45° angle. You're almost taking four steps to go one step. Mom and I started up it and I got about 80% up when I decided to stop, as I was starting to have trouble breathing. I'm a recovering asthmatic, probably about 90% recovered and it rarely ever bothers me anymore, but this was the sternest test I'd had and I really didn't want to push it since we were nowhere near medical attention. So Mom continued to the top while I came back down and waited for her. The majority of the people start at the dunes area when the gates open for two reasons-to see the sunrise effect and

get about two hours of cooler weather in. We climbed Dune 45 about 6:30 and although it was not hot yet, you could tell it wouldn't be long until that changed. After leaving the Dune, we drove a bit and then transferred to a safari vehicle which took us deeper into the landscape, where we walked around for an hour or so amongst the diverse landscape-sand, dry river beds, dry lake beds, dead trees, live trees, etc. We saw Big Daddy, which is the largest dune in Namibia and one of the largest in the world. After that we jumped into another vehicle which took us even further in and more scenery, including a lonely oryx standing there up a dune in front of us. After that was done, Mom and I thought that might be the end of the day's activity, but Agies told us he had another place he wanted to show us on the way back to the Homestead, and that was Sesriem Canyon. We spent almost an hour there, walking down to the bottom of it and then back up. It wasn't very deep but nice rock formations and there was even some standing water at the very bottom of it left over from a flash flood that had nowhere to go, and boy did it stink, I can still smell it! After the canyon it was back to Homestead (it was about noon by this time, and as we passed Dune 45 this time, nobody was climbing it-it was definitely too hot by now). We arrived back about 1:00 PM but having been up since so early, it already had been a full day, especially with the heat being so noticeable the last three hours or so. When journeying around that area, it is important to take a backpack of some sort and have at least two or three bottles minimum of bottled water, as once you get past the entry gate, there is absolutely no place to buy water or anything else. We relaxed the rest of the afternoon and I had sand all over me from waist down and naturally that was the only place we stayed that didn't have hot water. So my shower consisted of from the waist down. Agies joined us for dinner that evening. I can't remember what the main course was, but the important thing was that this time there were NO BEETS!! =:-) It was a very nice place to stay for two nights, and like our previous lodges, the staff was very, very friendly and accommodating.

Friday, September 4

We left Sossusvlei in the morning to head back to Windhoek, where we would spend our last couple of nights. It was about a 4-1/2 hour trip and once again the only sign of civilization until we got there would be Solitaire, this time about an hour into the journey. The road was primarily gravel again until reaching the outskirts of Windhoek. We could've taken a more direct route that would've passed us through a town called Rehoboth, but Agies decided to take us on an even more back-ways one, over a very high and steep mountain pass called Spreetshoogte (7300 feet/2220 meters high), which we appreciated, as we never would have found it ourselves since the road was barely on the map. And as evidence we saw even less traffic than the route between Swakopmund and Sossusvlei-this time it took us nearly 1-1/2 hours to encounter our second car. We arrived in Windhoek early afternoon where Agies dropped us off at the Steiner, where we'd stay the final two nights and where I'd stayed my first night there. We said goodbye to him and thanked him for being such an expert, friendly guide and an excellent driver (later on Mom and I each e-mailed the company he works for, to compliment them on Agies). The hotel is located just a couple blocks from the downtown area and I wanted to get a few more wooden artifacts as did Mom, so after a brief rest, we walked over to a crafts shop she was familiar with, that had everything priced and involved no dickering, and upon comparison I saw that I did okay with my negotiating in Swakopmund, except of course for that stupid nut. It was about N$45, so I guess the personal engraving was worth about $55 for that two seconds it took them to carve my name into it. Walking around Windhoek was fine as long as everything was kept hidden in pockets or a money- belt. It's just like any other place where you take precautions even though 99% of the people are fine. What scared me the most were the drivers! It seems to be "open season" on pedestrians and you almost need about twelve sets of eyes all around your head. When you're waiting to cross the street and the pedestrian "go" flashes green, if cars that want to turn think they can make it before you step onto the street, they'll go, or else they don't think it's unusual to get within a couple feet of you before they stop and let you continue on. And the green "go" tends to turn to red after about four seconds, in which the drivers get the idea that since it's not red anymore, it's their turn. But we learned to wait to cross with a local between us and the turning cars, and whenever the local would cross, then we felt safe to do so also. The rest of the day we decided to stay at the hotel, so we had another unhealthy but convenient KFC dinner and brought it back to the Steiner where we sat and ate it by the pool and talked for a couple of hours. That evening in the room I watched the Namibian News just for something interesting and different to do. The biggest stories dealt with the upcoming presidential election in November and the fact that a Namibian was selected to be on this upcoming season's "Big Brother Africa"!

Saturday, September 5
For my final full day in Namibia, we had breakfast and then by 10:00 AM it was time to play "dodge ball" with the cars once more and do some more shopping on Independence Avenue, the shopping area of Windhoek, about four blocks from the hotel, and definitely the gathering place of the people. Independence Avenue used to be known as Kaiser Avenue back in the days when Namibia was possessed by the Germans. It was extremely crowded walking down the street and especially in the mall, but that was because on the weekends, all the stores close for the day at 1:00 PM. We had a bite to eat in a little ice cream/sandwich shop in the mall and it was very interesting for me to just watch all the people go by. All the people, young and old, are dressed very nicely, even in their casual clothes, and there was no "gangsta" wear. And despite there being a lot of poor people in the country (especially up in Mom's area), everyone seemed to have a cell-phone. We had signed up for a four-hour afternoon van tour of the city and were back in time for that. The tour was very interesting, the guide very knowledgeable about the city and Namibia in general. He drove us to places such as the first building in Windhoek (from 1890), a landmark church, the parliament building and grounds, railroad station as well as the wealthiest parts of town to the shanty area. The driver emphasized that all areas of the city should be shown, not just the more well-to-do and historic areas. As for the shanty area, known as Katutura, a lot of the "shacks" have emerged just in the last couple of months as there is no social housing in the city since the government will not build it for fear of word getting out to the rest of Namibia (and Africa) that it's there and people can come to Windhoek and "live for free". In these poor areas, there are over 1,800 tiny, ramshackle bars lined up next to each other, all of them with a pool table in the middle of them and several people standing outside of them drinking and waving to us and inviting us in. So even though it was an impoverished area, at no time did it feel unsafe. In any case I appreciated the driver showing us all parts of the city and not wanting to sweep any part of it "under the rug". That evening Mom made reservations for us to have dinner at Joe's Beer House, which is THE place to go in Windhoek. You are totally engulfed in an African setting there with a jungle-like atmosphere and African decor all over the place. Even the bar area had its unusual charm, as the bar stools are actually old out-of-commission toilet seats! Our table for two was a long one, so another "table for two" sat with us, which is what they do there. We had dinner with a couple of very nice young Swiss ladies who'd just arrived and were really going to be winging

it for their four weeks in the country, as they had a rental car reserved but only one overnight accommodation booked for their entire stay. We had a really nice conversation with them and I told them that when they picked up their rental car the next day to be sure it had a jack in it! For my meal, I had a plate of oryx, springbok and ostrich. It was all very good but I couldn't tell which was which, as it tasted similar.

Sunday, September 6
This was the day for me to say 'goodbye' to Namibia and for Mom to return to Ondangwa (she would leave a few hours after me). My flight on SAA took off out of Windhoek at 12:30 PM for Johannesburg (where I would transfer to Air France for the Paris and then Seattle legs) so the shuttle was at the hotel at 9:30 to pick me up. It was another great flight on SAA with excellent service again. Amongst our passengers were the Swaziland National Soccer team, which had been in Windhoek the day before to play a match against Namibia, I'm assuming it had some sort of World Cup implications (by the way, the World Cup will be held in South Africa this upcoming June). It was kind've fun being on the plane with them, and they were all dressed in their jerseys. (Swaziland borders South Africa to the east.) They were very well-behaved and did start to get a little loud at the very end of the trip but by no means was it irritating, it was more entertaining than anything. I got the impression that some of them had hardly ever flown before by the way they were reacting to things, such as turbulence. After arriving in J'burg, I had a four-hour layover before I had to catch the flight to Paris, so I walked around the airport, which I was familiar with from the week before, and I bought a couple things I'd seen then also. I then boarded the flight for Paris, and as everyone was seat-belted in just before take-off, they made an announcement that they would now be coming through to spray the cabin for mosquitoes. Not sure if this is an Air France policy or for any flight leaving South Africa, but in any case the flight attendants walked down each aisle, each one holding two cans of spray and keeping their fingers on the trigger as they walked all the way down. The smell was virtually odorless and nobody complained, not even the French. But I'm sure they wouldn't have done it if it was unsafe. I did kind've wonder why they waited until everyone was on the plane and buckled in, but I guess it was because they wanted to make sure nobody nor their carry-on was hiding any of the little critters. After touching down in Paris I had another four-hour layover, so my layovers were about 11 hours less altogether than they were on the way over. And

like in J'burg, I bought some things in Paris that I'd seen the week before. And I got on the internet there and first thing I did like the addict I am was log on to 'facebook'. Eventually we took off to Seattle and 33 hours after leaving Windhoek, we touched down at Sea-Tac. Although it's always nice to get home, I did have a wonderful trip and for the eight days that I was there, Mom planned an outstanding itinerary, there is no way I could have done better. And as for the animal experience, we saw just about every one, except for a hippopotamus and the really elusive cheetah. I've felt pretty good ever since and as for jet lag, I didn't have any on the trip there, and when I arrived home, maybe two hours at the most, crashing for bed early and then getting up early. I guess if I was going to have it, I'd prefer everything to be "early" instead of "late".

Some more miscellaneous information about Namibia:
--Until 1920, it was a German colony (except for Walvis Bay which was controlled by the British) known as German South West Africa.
--In 1920, the League of Nations mandated the country to South Africa, and it was known as South West Africa.
--In 1990, the country claimed full independence, adopting the name Namibia after the Namib Desert, which stretches along the entire coastline.
--The population is only 2,100.000. It has the second lowest population density of any sovereign country (Mongolia is first). As a comparison, Great Britain is 25% of the size of Namibia but has 30 times more people.
--Namibia is the only country in the world to specifically address conservation and protection of natural resources in its constitution.
-The unemployment rate is 30-40%. *(Norene's note***the figures I heard were 20 to 25% but I think it depends on what the source is --anyway it is HIGH)*
--Mining is the #1 industry. Diamonds were traditionally the biggest item mined (the government is still a 50% shareholder in the diamond industry), but now it is uranium.
--The official language is English.
--The Namibian Dollar and South African Rand have the exact same value and are used interchangeably in the country. Usually if you pay for something in Rand, your change will be in Namibian money. However, Namibian money is not accepted in South Africa.
--Depending upon whom you talk to, Windhoek is either pronounced

"VIN-took", "WIN-took", or "WIN-dook". The "white" people tend to pronounce it with the "V" while the black Africans mainly use the "W".
--Eco-tourism is a rapidly growing industry, however there are still very few Americans there, probably because of the distance. When I would tell people where I was from, they all knew of the U.S.A., but very few of them knew of Seattle. Germans and South Africans seemed to be the majority of tourists, and there are even non-stop flights to Windhoek from Germany while coming from every other non-African country you pretty much have to go through Johannesburg first.
--The country still maintains very close ties with South Africa and has no tanks or planes in their military.

Norene and Elia with Himba ladies

Beautiful Himba children

Norene and Brad climbing Dune 45, Sesriem, Namibia

Riding camels outside of Swakopmund, Namibia

Some of the staff at Heroes School

Some of the staff at Heroes Private School in Ondangwa

More of the staff at Heroes School

IN AND AROUND NORTHERN NAMIBIA AND WINDING DOWN

Chapter 17--September-November, 2009

Our school had a Beauty Pageant/Talent show to choose Miss Heroes School of 2009 in September. The contestants were girls from the 8th and 9th grade. Six of my grade 5 girls performed a few somewhat synchronized dance numbers which they choreographed themselves. Most of the learners like to sing, dance and act. Some boys did some very quick dancing individually or in a small group between the times when the beauty contestants were not marching around the stage in their different modes of dress. I bought two tickets for the event and one bag of cheese curls to support the cause. After about two hours I left because that was about all of the loud blasting music I could stand. The show went on for an hour after that.

A week later there was an Honor's Program for learners and parents on a Sunday afternoon which was well attended. There is a lot of emphasis put on making good grades and individual class ranking. The ranking number is put on the grade report sent home at the end of each term and each of the learners is anxious to see where he/she is and where everyone else ranks in the class. There were a number of certificates handed out for excellent work in almost every subject studied. I can imagine what a controversy all of this comparing and publishing of grades and rankings from kindergarten on up would cause in some schools in the States with all the "P.C.ers".

The first Saturday of October I participated in a "Fun Walk" of 6K with about fifty others "60 years or older". It was out on a country road with police escort although there was very little traffic at 6:00 AM. The weather is delightfully cool at that hour and it was fun walking through the countryside. I thought it would be go for a walk and then go home but it was a "wellness clinic" on ways to keep healthy. At one place during the walk I came up beside this gentleman who turned to me and asked, "How is your knee?" This gave me a little start wondering how he would know about that, then I recognized him as Dr. B., my physical therapist. I hadn't recognized him in his sports clothes. I told him I was doing well with a lot of thanks to him.

After the walk we all sat on chairs in a circle under some large shade trees listening to some talks about healthy eating, exercising, weight control and coping with stress. (I really thought these people did not experience stress with their life style, but apparently some do.) Then we were weighed and measured for height so the two nurses could figure out each person's BMI-Body Mass Index-which they wrote on individual little cards. I think there may have been five or six of us who were of normal weight and all the rest were overweight by a few pounds/kilograms to many kilograms. These are those people who have more money to eat more, have cars and don't walk as much as the majority of the population does, I would judge. Upon receiving my BMI card the nurse told me that my number is too low so I needed to gain 3 kg (6.6 pounds) in order to reach the acceptable minimum of 18. This was the first time in my whole life that I was told that I need to gain weight. I think she measured and weighed me incorrectly. At any rate I didn't try to gain any weight. This activity was sponsored by the Public Hospital and most of the participants were hospital workers, I was told by the man who transported me to and from the event. There was another Fun Walk the first Saturday of November which I did not attend because I was involved in preparing for my "Thank You" parties which I'll get to later. I saw Kathindi (the man who drove me to the first walk) at a store in town after that one; he told me there were only twelve there in November but they were going to meet and decide when the next one would be.

On the weekend of October 10, several of my World Teach colleagues gathered at one of the teacher's homes farther north from Ondangwa to celebrate Canadian Thanksgiving. That time fit into everyone's schedule better than the U.S. Thanksgiving date when some of the group would be leaving Namibia on that weekend for home or travel before returning to their homes. There were 3 Canadians, 7 Americans, and 4 Namibians so it was an International happening. Steve, another Canadian, had already left for a new job as a regional director of a NP educational organization which was just starting in South Africa, but we did enjoy the turkey which he provided. His turkey was in Ogongo but he was in Johannesburg. We ladies wore our Meme (muumuu) dresses for the dinner. We all stayed overnight because of the difficulty of getting transportation back home at night to our various villages. One of the Canadian gals, Jen, provided "crackers" (a Canadian custom) which is like a party favor that has a little gift and saying inside that is used at Christmas mainly, I believe. I was not familiar with this custom at all. Anyway on the count of three everyone pulls both ends of the cracker and out pop the little goodies from inside. She found them at one of the stores (our favorite Game store) in Oshakati which amazes me that they would have such a foreign thing. Maybe the Namibians use them, as well.

World Teach's End of Service meeting was on the weekend of October 23 for three days. We were transported to and from our homes/schools to the town of Otjiwarongo, about a four to five hour drive south of my village. Our accommodations were pretty good. We stayed at a guest house this time and the meals were catered or at a restaurant rather than being prepared in the hostel kitchen as before some of the times. Actually we had meetings just on Saturday so it was more of a fun relaxing time this time. We did have to play a few silly games which I don't like and later found that some of the younger volunteers didn't like them either. I thought it was just me, being "Meme Kuku" that had this feeling. The one couple who are "seniors" wasn't there; I don't know why, so I was really the "granny" of the group. After the dinner on Saturday night everyone received a very creative award thought up by our Field Director and her assistant, for something accomplished this year. Mine was the Survivor Award. I think it was because of my "soldiering on" when I had the cast on for six weeks during the flood season and didn't even consider going home. Actually I thought everyone deserved an award for surviving the year. There were five people who were extending for the next year. More power to them! One young man had already been here for two years but he moved to another school close to where his girlfriend was. They became a "couple" this year; I think this happened during the flood season when both of their schools were closed for almost six weeks.

In October we had a few very healthy thunder and lightning storms which cooled things off a bit. I enjoyed hearing the rain on the metal roof at night this time since there wasn't a foot of water already on the ground as earlier in the year. October, November and December are the really HOT months, we were told, and I do believe this. It was a delightful 65-70 degrees F in the morning but it started warming up around 10:00 AM and by mid afternoon it was 95-100 degrees. I "mosquito-proofed" my windows which I should have done much earlier with mosquito netting on the inside held with double-stick tape and bricks on the window sills to hold the netting down. This way I could close the windows when needed; a smarter person could have figured this out earlier. I didn't have to close the windows at night in order to keep the mosquitoes and other little beasties out. It made a world of difference and I didn't have to sleep with the fan on all night as before. I woke up to the cool refreshing air. Martha Stewart probably would have been aghast at this arrangement, but it worked for me.

A few weekends later, I went with four of the young gals down to Tsumeb to see what the annual Copper Festival was all about. We were hoping to buy a few copper things to take back home but there wasn't a piece of copper to buy. There is a big copper mine a little north-east of Tsumeb; there was one booth that told and showed the history of the mining industry. There were lots of booths selling cheap junk like at many street fairs but there were some that had cheap to fairly good African crafts. I succumbed and bought a few more things. The festival was held in a very large park and lots of people attended. There were many *braais*-barbeques-and beer drinking, as well as soft drinks and a few healthy foods to eat, loud music and dancing on the grass with all of the many people having a good time. Being with the four young women, I readily saw how they got "hit upon" all the time by the young men. I think they handled it pretty well; they've had to because the men are very persistent. We stayed in a hostel a few blocks from the park and six of our other colleagues were there as well, so we had another little reunion. We always had a good time together no matter who was in the group.

Backing up a bit--the four others met at my place on Friday afternoon because they picked up the rental car in Ondangwa, my village. Rachel drove the car and did a good job. She had driven a few other times to various places especially when her mother was with her for three months. The traffic travels on the left side of the road rather than the right so it takes some getting used to. The plan was to camp because we couldn't get reservations for the dorm rooms. The girls had 2-4 person tents and 1 single tent so they decided to leave one of the bigger tents at my house. We were off about 5:00 PM. They wanted to stop at some of the *shebeens/*

bars with the more colorful names to take pictures and maybe go in one or two. We didn't go in any; I really didn't want to because it was the end of the month when everyone has money to hang out drinking, playing pool and it gets quite rowdy, even though they are friendly. I'm glad the girls had second thoughts about it. Originally we thought there would be safety in numbers.

At the last little enclave of buildings where we drove just off the main highway, when we were looking at the names and not paying much attention to the road surface (actually there wasn't any road surface) we got stuck in the sand. Almost immediately about four or five young men came up to the car. Jen and Rachel who were in the front seat asked if they could give us a push. They said they would for $50; we said, "No". Then they said they would for $30 and the answer was still, "No." Four of us decided to get out and push which we did and after a few minutes the car did move forward and Rachel drove about the distance of half a block to get on firmer ground. While we were pushing, there were about a dozen men and a few ladies standing in a circle around the car watching this whole operation and laughing. The Namibians love to laugh at anyone's misfortune. So much for male chivalry-there isn't much as far as I observed. Actually I did have a few kindnesses bestowed upon me by taxi drivers and men in the stores. One thing that really bothered me with the learners during class time was when they laughed at another of the learners who made a mistake or gave the wrong answer. Of course, they see the adults do it all the time so why should I expect them to be any different?

It was after 9:00 PM when we arrived at the hostel and when unpacking the trunk they found there was only the single tent which they said I could have-since I'm the Meme Kuku, I suppose. Both of the 4-person tents were left at my house by mistake. There was some light out there in the back yard so we didn't have to operate completely in the dark. After getting things organized we walked to the park and were there for about two hours and were disappointed about not seeing any copper, but we had fun anyway. I had my sleeping bag but had sent my mat back home since I had never used it, so although I was warm enough, that ground was pretty hard. The four girls slept outside and two of them didn't have sleeping bags, just blankets, so they got pretty cold that night. The next morning we noticed that there were no people in the dorm rooms and were told they had cancelled out at the last minute so on Saturday night three of us opted to go into one of the dorm rooms, which was so much better. It cost $10 more but was well worth it. The other two slept outside in the tent.

On Saturday morning we went out for breakfast at an open-air restaurant where we had been before on another trip to Tsumeb, then walked around the town to look at the shops. I don't really like shopping that much unless there is something I really need or want to buy but the young gals enjoyed it and I enjoyed being with them. All of them live in much smaller villages than I do so the trip to a clean fairly large city **and** having a car instead of depending on public transport or walking was a welcome experience for all of us and since the stores close early on Saturdays we went back to the park for a while then back to the hostel for the afternoon just to rest and talk. That evening we went back to the park, walked around a bit and then just spread out a blanket and sat on it observing things. The girls had talked of going to a concert that night but decided not to in the end. I would have opted out of this because I just can't stand a lot of loud music (noise) for more than a short time. The next day we headed back and even though we were disappointed with the Copper Festival, with no copper, we had a nice weekend.

The second week of November I had my "Thank you parties" for grade 5, grade 7, and the staff. I wanted to have it all done before exams started because then the schedule (times table) gets all changed. I made cookies and bought some more cookies (biscuits) for the two grades; there are eighty in both classes together and made some punch for them. I invited each class over during their class period on the Monday before exams. I had my neighbor Marissa take pictures of both classes with me in them, about two weeks before and had a print made for each learner because they always wanted a print of whatever was taken, however this was the first I actually did it. There is a store uptown called Magic Discounters which sells everything under the sun but they have the Kodak machine which will make prints from camera cards, CD's and cell phones, like the drugstores at home have. The young man who is in charge can do everything so fast; i.e. enhancing, cropping and all the rest so the customer doesn't have to do anything but stand, wait and then pay. The charge for each print is $3.50 N which is about 45 cents U.S. but at this time they were having a special price of $3 because of Christmas. The forty-three 7th graders did fit in my living/kitchen area; I had wondered about this.

The staff party was on Wednesday after school and once again it was "snack, unhealthy food" but everyone seemed to enjoy it. I made two chocolate cakes for them which I served with ice cream, then there were cookies, cheese, crackers, and chips. For drinks I had wine, beer, soda, and juice. There were twenty for this and all fitted pretty comfortably in my kitchen/living room for this. John Carlo brought chairs from the library so they all had a place to sit in a big circle. They ate and drank most of it and what was left over they wrapped up and took with them. Actually, they began doing this when everyone started getting up to leave without my asking if they wanted to take something with them. I did want them to take all the left-overs because I didn't want any of it left there for me; this way I wouldn't be tempted. I thanked them for their acceptance of me and all their help; then one of the staff, the person I had earlier had strong disagreements with about discipline, got up and made some kind remarks about me on behalf of the staff. So there were no hard feelings over this. One thing they would remember about me is that Miss Norene made learners give me their shoe if they borrowed a pen until I got the pen back. The staff thought this was really funny. As I stated before, there were a few learners who refused to do this so they didn't get a pen; then I made them come over and sit on the floor by my table to write the lesson. They didn't like this of course, but I couldn't let them get the best of me. You would think I had asked them to cut off their arm--a slight exaggeration.

In the store in mid-November, I heard "Jingle Bells" and "It's Beginning To Look A lot Like Christmas" as the "canned" background music which surprised me because I hardly thought of Christmas there because the weather was so hot and although there were a few "Christmassy" things in the stores, it certainly was not like back home which, I think, has really gotten out of hand for a long time. The workers in some of the stores were wearing Santa Claus hats.

The year was winding down very quickly and those last few weeks were very busy with exams, recording marks, filling out other papers, getting rid of personal things and packing for home and for my last few weeks of travel in Africa before flying back to the States. Although I was very much looking forward to being home it was quite emotional saying good-bye to the learners and staff members knowing that I probably wouldn't be seeing them again. A number of the 5th graders had been telling me weeks before that they were going to come home with me. A few people in the stores occasionally indicated they wanted to go to America with me. On two occasions earlier in the year, one in a store and the other in the doctor's office, I was asked about my family. When I said I have two sons, one married and the other single, both times one of the ladies said they would like to marry my son. When I questioned them about already being married (noting the wedding ring on the left hand) I was told, "Oh. I can divorce my husband so I can marry your son." I said I didn't know what my son would think about that. It was especially "teary" with the 5th graders and some of the 7th graders. Two of the boys from grade 5, who absolutely gave me "fits" especially during Term 1, seemed to be sad to see me leaving. They were both good children but didn't seem to give a "rip" about learning and/or following classroom rules; I thought if my hair doesn't turn gray dealing with these two, maybe it never will. At any rate from about the middle of the year on, we became "friends" and by the end of the year they couldn't do enough for me. I felt this was one of my successes. The advantage of teaching and being there for a year gave me an opportunity to learn a lot about the country and the people there. This is one of the reasons I chose to volunteer in this capacity.

LEAVING ONDANGWA AND VISITING SOUTH AFRICA AND TANZANIA

Chapter 18 – December 2009

On the morning of Wednesday, December 2, three of the teachers took me to the little airport outside of Ondangwa for the 1½ hour flight (by turbo-prop) to Windhoek, the capital. As we were driving out of the school grounds, some staff and learners were still saying good-bye and I received a few more gifts. I spent two days in the city before I would board the Intercape Sleepliner for Cape Town, an eighteen hour ride.

While in the city for two days, I packed and mailed two more boxes home, did a little shopping, and took a safari to a cheetah reserve about an hour's drive out of the city to see the cheetahs up close from the safari vehicle while they were being fed. First the guide threw out raw chicken necks for the appetizer, I presume. There were six cheetahs altogether. They kind of fought over the meat but they all got some. Of course, the people in the vehicles were watching and taking pictures like crazy. Then the next course was beef bones about a foot long with meat on them; this time when one of them caught a bone in its mouth it would go off a little ways to chew/gnaw it in peace. Finally all six got their treats, one at time and were happily chewing away when we left; they performed well for us.

On my last night in Windhoek, I went back to Joe's Beer House for an "African type meal" and to buy a tee shirt for Brad that we couldn't get when he was visiting me. This time I had zebra and it was very good. The next night I boarded the Intercape Sleepliner for the eighteen hour trip to Cape Town. The bus left about two hours late from Windhoek because it was waiting on a bus from Johannesburg and one from Swakopmund that had passengers who had reservations for Cape Town. The ride was comfortable but I couldn't sleep very much plus a had a very large seatmate who took up one-third of my space. There wasn't an arm rest to put down between us. The bus made a number of stops along the way to let off and pick up passengers but only for a few minutes. There were a few longer rest stops where we could get off for fifteen to twenty minutes to go to the restroom and get something to eat and/or drink. Some of the people had done the trip before and knew the routine, so I would ask them if we were to get off the bus or stay on it.

We arrived at the South African border about 5 or 6 A.M. where we went through departure and then immigration about twenty-five minutes later. A visa is not required so it was a simple procedure but at immigration there was only one agent, so it took quite a long time for everyone to get through because the agent had to look at the passport and the computer screen for something before stamping the passport. At any rate we were on our way once again. We passed through some very pretty green areas in northern South Africa where irrigation is used. Other scenery consisted of higher rocky mountains and lower mountains, some pretty barren areas, bush veld and desert. In the farther south there were more towns, flatter land and more vegetation.

Cape Town, South Africa

Arrival time in Cape Town, South Africa was about 3:30 P.M. instead of 1:30 P.M. By the time we were nearing the transit station almost all of the people had gotten off the bus. There was still a middle-aged couple on and they and the attendant on the bus were concerned about me traveling alone so when we arrived at the terminal, they helped me get a "reliable" taxi to take me to the hostel where I had reservations. The station was like a beehive with people arriving and departing on all manner of buses and trains.

This Backpack Hostel is probably the nicest one I've ever been in. I always opt for a single room because even though I can get along with almost everyone, I like to have "my things" in a locked room when I go out. At this time I was traveling with two large roller suitcases and two backpacks. Primrose at reception was very helpful in getting me settled and later setting up tours for me on Sunday and Tuesday. The first thing I wanted to do was have a shower and wash my sweaty clothes that I had been in for the greater part of two days. The hostel had a nice restaurant and open patio area; the sun was shining and there was a gentle breeze so I really felt relaxed and at last I was in the beautiful city of Cape Town. From one of the patios there was an excellent view of Table Mountain which dominates the city from many places. I made the reservations for Cape Town and Johannesburg through Acacia Africa which conducts camping trips mainly from seven days to two months but they do advertise a few city tours such as I was doing.

On Sunday I took the Red Bus City Tour which has a number of stops at points of interest where passengers can get off and spend as much or as little time as they desire, then take the next bus that comes along. My first stop was at Table Mountain which was good because even though there were quite a number of people there, it wasn't as crowded as it would be later on. It was a lovely clear day and not very hot. I took the cable car to the top like most people did and observed the beautiful view from there of two beaches, parts of the city and the ocean. After going back down to the other area, I rejoined the Red Bus which went down to the central city part for more of the circle city tour. I didn't get off any place but just enjoyed sitting there on the top floor of the double deck bus looking at the beautiful beaches and buildings. We were given earphones to listen to the commentary in whatever language we chose, as we traveled along, about all the points of interest.

Next day was the Peninsula Cape Tour by touring van which consisted of several different activities. First, after driving about an hour, was a boat ride out of Hout Bay to observe many seals on one of the islands and then on to Boulders where beautiful black and white African Penguins (formerly called Jackass Penguins) are nested in the vegetation along the shore where they can easily go out to the water to catch the fish. Next we had a bike ride for about twelve kilometers along the coastline to our picnic spot; here we saw a number of baboons who can be quite aggressive. I did not know there would be bike riding until I first went out to the van and saw a dozen bikes in the trailer; I was a bit apprehensive about this since I hadn't been on a bike for about two years but was determined to give it a try with the six younger people on the tour; I did manage alright with a little help from the others in getting started after I figured out the gears. After lunch it was back on the bikes for about an eight kilometer ride down to Cape Point, the most southwestern part of Africa. Along the way there were more baboons being herded along by two park people. We were warned to keep moving and not spend time taking pictures; of course, as usual some people paid no attention to this. There were a number of other small tour groups. There were two steep hikes up to view points. The day had started out with rain but it cleared off nicely by mid-morning and the rest of the time it was a combination of blue sky, sun and white fluffy clouds. I loved the whole day; I did wonder if I would be able to get out of bed the next day with the biking and hiking but there were no residual affects, fortunately.

The next day another tour took us out to a few of the "townships" as they are called to see how the people live. The townships developed during the apartheid era to separate the population into white, colored and black groups. Housing runs from very dilapidated shacks to some that are more substantial. On all the tours the guides spoke of the history of the apartheid era. In one place we visited a "medicine man's" shop. There were all kinds of animal dried parts, skins, and bones on tables and hanging from the ceiling. Some items were completely unrecognizable to me. The medicine man was working in the back room. As I understand it, he works when he gets an inner feeling that "this is the time" to make his medicines and potions. You might say he works "when the spirits move him to do so." After a time the smell got to me so I went outside to get fresh air.

Next I was dropped off at the pier for the boat ride out to Robben Island where Nelson Mandela was incarcerated for many years. It was the maximum prison for South African political prisoners and the black and colored murderers; the whites were sent to Pretoria during that time. Upon leaving the boat we were herded into buses for a tour around the grounds. The buildings are made of rock and are standing on rock. Ex-prisoners are the guides. Our guide was a financial person working in Angola and South Africa and was convicted for some kind of what you would say is a white-collar crime; he probably was accused falsely (just my opinion). He was intelligent, articulate and seemed to hold no rancor. He related quite a bit about Nelson Mandela and his cell was pointed out to us. This was another very interesting day.

The next day was my last day in this beautiful city of Cape Town. I had the travel desk at the hostel book a half day tour out to the wine country east of the city for me since I was leaving in late afternoon for Johannesburg. I originally thought I wouldn't do the wine tasting tour because I have been to a number of wineries in the U.S. and other places, but I had several free hours before having to leave for the Sleepliner Bus and I did want to see the beautiful countryside so off I went. The scenery was magnificent with flat green country and rolling hills. This was almost summer time so there were lovely flowers, shrubs, green trees and the vineyards. It was fun being with the others who were on the tour from various countries–Germany, Sweden, England, France and the U.S.

Johannesburg, South Africa

The Sleepliner left about 7 PM instead of 5:30 PM–this was Africa where hardly anything happens on schedule. The bus was comfortable but I just have a hard time sleeping anywhere unless I'm lying down flat. I did sleep a few hours with the aid of a sleeping pill. The terrain we passed that day going into Johannesburg was mostly flat and green; there had been rain off and on for about month. We arrived at the transit station about 4:15 PM instead of 1:30 so it had been about twenty-four hours since I had first arrived at the station back in Cape Town. The reason I had opted to take the bus these two times is because my airplane ticket from Victoria Falls to Windhoek earlier in May had cost nearly $500 U.S. so I thought it would be about the same, but learned too late, that the flights would have been just a little bit more that the bus tickets, oh well, I did see the countryside. Once more, someone was looking after me, because the bus hostess was concerned about my traveling alone and where I was going next so she arranged my transport to the next hostel. This was the Backpacker Ritz; it is in a nice residential part of Johannesburg but it wasn't my idea of the "Ritz" although it was clean and the people were very nice and friendly there.

Since I reserved a single room of which there were none, I presume, I had three beds but I managed to fill most of them. I had three small bags which I planned to take on my two week trip, but I had two larger suitcases that I mentioned before, which I would leave in Johannesburg at the hotel where I would be staying the last night and pick up when I returned from Tanzania to fly back to the States.

The one tour I signed up for was to the township of Soweto; I felt I could not visit Johannesburg with out seeing this area, the place we've heard about mainly because of Nelson Mandela and Bishop Tutu. There were only two people on this: one younger man and me, but we did the whole thing. First we went to the transport and big market area. I was pleasantly surprised by the homes that were built for the people when apartheid went into effect. These, for the most part, were made of brick with metal roofs and they are being replaced by better quality homes as money becomes available. There were some "shack-type", however. I mentioned before that I had seen very substandard homes in Cape Town and earlier back in Namibia in the Katutura area of Windhoek. There are four million people in Soweto with the poor, middle class and upper class there. At one place we left the van to make a loop walk through the neighborhood. A number of children, probably twenty, ran up to meet us and hung on for dear life. Apparently they know that tourists will stop there at times. They were very exuberant and loving; they wanted candy. They wanted to feel my hair, (the children in Namibia were the same). My partner said he wouldn't buy them candy but would buy them fruit, so we stopped at an outdoor stand where a lady was selling fruit. He made sure that each child had an apple or a banana and then paid her 20 Rand, I believe, (about $3 US); I offered to pay but he said, "No." They walked with us back up to the main street. When you see children like this who virtually have nothing, the pain goes straight to your heart, especially when they are talking, laughing and loving you.

Our next stop was at the Hector Petierson Museum. This is in conjunction with the Day of the African Child about which I wrote earlier. To review, there was a student protest on June 16, 1976 here in Johannesburg which was organized at one school but spread to other schools which joined in and it was broadcast around the world. There were hundreds of students killed by the police and many injured, as I understand it. This museum was built in remembrance of that whole situation. It was very interesting and very well done. It was enlightening to read some of the policemen's recollections of the events compared to what the students, families, and teachers wrote of the whole happening. This experience at the museum and thinking about the whole situation is one I will not soon forget. While in Soweto we did see the homes of Nelson Mandela and Bishop Tutu; they are just a block or so apart.

Lastly we visited a neighborhood shebeen/bar nearby for that experience; this was at 11 AM. The three of us and three other men were the only ones in the bar; the walls were painted very brightly with scenes of a band and people having a good time that I could imagine depicting what might happen in New Orleans during Mardi Gras, although I've never been there. I don't know how these tiny little places of business survive but they seem to.

The next day I moved to a hotel somewhat near the airport which my son had suggested and it was very nice. I had a three-room suite with a huge bathtub. I had a "guilty pleasure" by taking a nice long soaking bath in this huge bathtub. Much of Africa has a problem with water but I decided to have this bath anyway especially after my short lukewarm showers/baths in Namibia. The hotel was in a very pretty residential part of the city. I had contacted my very good friend Colleen, who lives in an area near this city, the day before. This was really the main reason I wanted to spend a little time in Johannesburg. She and her family came to get me in the evening and we had a very good dinner and social time at a Dutch/Indonesian Restaurant, somewhere in the area. Colleen's daughter lives in Bellingham north of where I live and we've been friends for many years; it was so much fun to reconnect and meet some of the rest of her family.

Tanzania

On Sunday I went to the airport to start the second half of this journey; i.e. going to Tanzania. I just had my three small bags so it was easier traveling. It was about a three hour flight from Johannesburg to Dar es Salaam which is the capital of Tanzania. It is one of the major entry ports to that country. I knew I had to have a visa for this country but I got mixed messages from the Internet (my only form of communication whilst in Namibia) saying that I had to have one before I entered the country and another saying that I could get it at the airport when I arrived, plus some people in South Africa told me the latter. As it turned out I did get it at the airport for $100 along with many other people. I met four young Peace Corps workers while I was in line. They were stationed in Zimbabwe teaching at a teacher's college and had come to climb Mt. Kilimanjaro. They were curious about how old I was. I finally told them the truth and they started equating me to their grandparents as most of the young people I met during the year did.

I took a taxi to the Royal Mirage Hotel, this was about 9:30 PM and as the taxi driver drove into the street where the hotel was, I thought, "Norene, what have you gotten yourself into?" because the street was potholed and dirt with young and old men sitting on the sides just looking, plus I couldn't see any building that looked like a hotel, but we did come to the hotel sandwiched in between other buildings, piles of dirt and brick piles. The taxi driver charged me $30 US although it was supposed to be $20. The hotel manager wouldn't help me out with the price. I thought, oh well, live and learn. I do know that those service people do need the money more than I do and I always want to pay a fair price but I don't like to be taken advantage of. The hotel was fine–the budget type which I usually opt for. There was a thunder and lightning storm during the night with claps of thunder louder than I have ever heard. In the morning there was a lot of water that had come in from under the door that went out to the little balcony.

The next morning I took a walk down to the main street to find an ATM machine to get Tanzanian shillings. Here the exchange rate was about 1350 Tanzanian shillings to $1 US. I noticed that all side streets off of the main paved street were dirt. Once again there were many men sitting around by the sides of every street; this was the case in Namibia, as well. I surmise this is the case because of the high unemployment rate, the men don't have a job and the women are home taking care of the home, children, tending animals and crops if they have enough land to grow things. I left the hotel about 9:30 for the airport; this time we agreed on the price of $20 before I left the hotel. The airport is rather quiet and small for an international airport.

There were not many people for Arusha where I was going. We couldn't land at Arusha because of the weather so went to Kilimanjaro International Airport then boarded a bus for Arusha. It was about an hour's drive which gave us a chance to see the countryside. The feature I noticed about the landscape was the profusion of bananas plants and the lushness of the land. I suppose this made an impression on me because it is so very different from Namibia. Also, I saw the men pushing or pulling very large carts with all manner of products on them including: sticks for firewood and fencing, bananas, sugar cane, grass, water containers and vegetable produce. At times someone was pushing while another person was pulling. Cattle were the beast of burden most of the time, whereas in Namibia it was donkeys.

The bus took us to the square where my hotel, The New Safari Hotel, was which was fortunate for me so I didn't have to take a taxi anywhere. When I went to check in, the receptionist told me I had no reservation. Mind you, I had made the reservation in July and it was paid for. She wasn't very friendly but about fifteen minutes later she told me not to worry because if they couldn't take me at their hotel, they would get me a room in some other hotel, but as it turned out I did stay at this hotel because someone had found my reservation. It was a nice hotel and the personnel were helpful. They put me in touch with a travel agent to arrange for tours for the next two days.

The next morning I went to Moshi which is the town where climbers start for the climb of Mt. Kilimanjaro. I knew I couldn't climb the mountain but I wanted to see it while I was in Africa. This was not the best time because it is the rainy season but I was hoping for a glimpse. It took about two hours to get there from Arusha. While driving there, we did see the top for about a half hour; it was in the distance (I don't know how far away) although it was cloudy; there was snow on the top. We passed several villages on the way with markets of produce and other items for sale. There were many people out and once again many men just seemingly sitting around. Gideon, my guide, said that unemployment is at about 40%. We went up to the entrance where climbers register. I walked around for about thirty minutes and then went up to the staging area. I wanted to walk up a little ways (just to say I had been on the trail) but the guard told me that I had to have a permit which I didn't have.

Gideon met a friend of his who took me to meet his family and see his home. I had mentioned to Gideon on the way there that I wanted to take a photo of a native home, but I was just thinking of stopping by the road to do it. At any rate, this young man, Saani, took me down a rather steep and rocky path through the "jungle" of vegetation which included banana, mango and coffee trees to his home. We went to his grandfather's home which was a mud hut with a very low doorway and stepped into the darkness inside. It was smoky because the cooking fire on one side of the room was smoldering. It was divided into two parts with the livestock in one side and Grandpa in the other. I don't know where he was. A man and women came into the huts; my guide, Saani, took pictures with my digital camera; he seemed to love to do this and at one point I wondered if I would get my camera back. Then he told me I should give them a gift. I told him I had no gifts but I did give them some money. Then we went outside and a whole gaggle of children appeared to have their picture taken, then Saani said I should give them money. I pulled out a $5000 shilling note and one boy "globbed" onto it really fast and held it tightly. I asked him to share it; he gave a slight nod.

Saani asked if I would like to try a banana and millet brew; I didn't really want to but he insisted. We stopped in another hut with two men inside; they gave me a plastic container containing about a pint of brew and asked me to drink it. I took two sips and then handed it to Saani and he drank the rest. It didn't taste too bad; it was rather grainy, but I knew I couldn't drink anymore. On the way back he took several snaps of me walking; I don't know why. At the top we did have our picture taken together. He said he hadn't worked for three months so didn't have enough money to feed his family and asked me to send money monthly to him for his family. I do feel sorry for these people but I can't send money to everyone who asked me which was quite a few. I did give him half of my lunch that the hotel had packed and the rest of my shillings. On the way back we stopped in Moshi so I could get money for the safari for the next day. I found that with a Visa ATM one can take out 800 K shillings but only 200 K at a time, so you can do it four times in succession one day but with a Master card one can only take out 200 K in one day.

The next day I was booked for a game safari in Arusha National Park. I really wasn't thinking of taking another game drive but I didn't want to just stay in the hotel or go around town for the day, but I really enjoyed it because I got to see thousands of pink and white flamingos rather closely which I had only seen in pictures before plus the one kind of monkey that is only in Tanzania, white-faced colobus. There were other animals in rather large groups including baboons, giraffe, zebra, warthogs, African or Cape buffalo and waterboks, but no elephants or lions although they are in the park.

On the way back to the hotel there was a lot of traffic. Maybe they have "commute traffic" there, as well; I don't know. On a number of the wagons there were huge piles of grass. Some of the people go out everyday to cut grass to feed their livestock. I asked Nixon, my driver, what livestock people have and he said, "Dogs." I think something must have gotten lost in the translation. I met a young woman, Melissa from South Carolina, on this day when we were watching the flamingos who was in Africa for a few weeks with visiting engineers teaching university students. On this day off she decided to take a little trip to see the countryside.

The next day I flew to Zanzibar which is right off the eastern coast of Tanzania. The flight was only about twenty-five minutes. I had made reservations at the Kendwa Breezes Beach Resort on the northwest coast. The hotel had made arrangements for my transport to and from Stone Town, the main city on the island. It was about an hour's drive from the airport; along the way we passed many coconut palms and banana trees, went through a number of villages and saw a lot of activity amongst the people. Zanzibar seems to be mainly Muslim judging from the women's and young girls' attire with the dresses covering most of their bodies and the scarves on their heads. The police stopped the taxi in one of the villages and asked the driver to get out of the car. His companion stayed in the car; I think he was just along for the ride. I asked if there was a problem? He told me, "No," but the police do stop cars, make the driver show papers and then make them pay money to proceed. It isn't legal but it is a common practice. When we left the main road we were on a very rough road going through the bush and sand dunes with no life or buildings in sight. Once again I thought I had made a mistake in booking something, but the taxi driver assured me that the hotel was nice and it was just over the hill.

It was a nice beach-side hotel but there had been no electricity on the entire island for two weeks and even though the hotel had generators, they were short on fuel. The petrol stations were charging three times the regular price, so for the two and a half days I was there, the electricity was only on for about two hours one night from about 11:00 PM until 1:00 AM and the water was off a goodly portion of the time. It was on for two hours in the morning and two hours in the evening. There was power in the restaurant because they did serve the meals but at night it was dining by candle light. It would have been romantic if I had had a partner there with me. Despite the inconveniences, it was a great place with a beautiful white sandy beach and the other amenities of a beachside resort. There were several other hotels along this beach. I was told that water and electricity shortages are not uncommon. There was something about the underwater cable coming from the mainland being broken and should have been repaired a few years back but nothing was done about it at that time. I took long walks on the beach in the mornings and late afternoons when the sun wasn't so hot. There was a breeze most of the time so the temperature was pleasant when one was outside. It was quite warm in the hotel room. I didn't sleep with the mosquito net on because this makes it even warmer; I didn't see or hear any mosquitoes.

On the last night in Zanzibar, I stayed in Stone Town, the capital, in order to be near the airport for my flight back to Dar es Salaam. I did have a chance to walk around in the afternoon and the next morning. The streets are very narrow and wind around between the tall buildings on both sides. The Chavda Hotel was comfortable and interesting with its Arab and Indian furnishings and large rooms with very high ceilings. I had the best pineapple that I've ever tasted in Tanzania. It was so sweet and juicy with no acid taste at all. I, also, had the whitest scrambled eggs that I have ever had while in that country. I chose to eat a boiled egg one morning at breakfast to see if the egg actually did have a yolk; it did but it was very pale. In Namibia, the yolks were the yellowest that I've ever seen. My flight back to Dar es Salaam was in the afternoon the next day so I had plenty of time for a very pleasant morning walk. There was a lot of activity down along the beach by the sea. There were many boats anchored out close to the shore. I don't know what the boats were being used for; some of them looked like houseboats.

The airport for my flight back to Dar es Salaam was a ten minute taxi ride from the hotel. I spent the night again at the Royal Mirage Hotel and then left early the next morning for the flight back to Johannesburg. It was an uneventful evening which was fine by me. This room had an even stranger shower set-up than the last room I was in. The shower was on one side of the bathroom but the drain for it was on the opposite side of the room. The floor was flat so the water had to travel across the room to reach the drain which resulted in the whole floor being wet, but it was a shower and had warm water. I left the next morning about 5:00 AM for the airport; it was very busy at this early hour mostly for people going to Johannesburg. The flight took about 3 ½ hours; they served a full breakfast with real tableware. We landed at 10:30 AM and I proceeded to get a taxi to take me back out to the Outlook Lodge to pick up my two regular bags which I had stored there. The taxi driver assured me he knew where the hotel was. I asked what the fare would be and was told by two people, him and his supervisor, that it would be on the meter. The driver had trouble finding the place even with the printed directions I gave him but after stopping to ask a few times we found it. When we arrived back at the airport I asked him what the meter showed and he said they didn't use the meter when going that far from the airport. I didn't think it was on because I couldn't see any numbers. It turned out to be $60 U.S.; I didn't argue with him but told him I thought it was too much, but I paid him; what else could I do?

Grade 7 class Heroes School

End of service for World Teach-October 2009

Children in Soweto Township, South Africa

With children at their home near Mt. Kilimanjaro, Tanzania

Norene in typical Namibian attire

THE LAST CHAPTER---
ARRIVING BACK HOME

Chapter 19--December 21 & 22, 2009

My flight back to Dulles International didn't leave until 6:00 PM so I had plenty of time; I went to check in at 1:00 PM, as I was instructed earlier to do. I was told by the agent that there was no ticket number on my e-ticket so I would have to pay $250 U.S. or 1900 rand because the ticket had been changed from the original. I knew that it was changed from the original round trip because a return trip cannot be scheduled a year in advance but it was changed in June by World Teach and the extra fee was paid. The agent talked to her superior who said the same thing, but she suggested I talk to him, which I did. After about ten minutes while he asked me a number of questions about the group I came with, what I was doing in Africa, where I had been and never looking at me even once, he finally relented and scribbled about twelve numbers on my e-ticket paper, and said I could check in. Later on when we were standing in line for the last security check waiting to board, two of the people in our original group of World Teach came to get in line; I didn't know they were going to be on the plane. I asked if they had the same problem; they did but they had to pay the $250 but were hoping to get their money back when they would contact the World Teach director in Cambridge, MA. There were a few others, I learned later, who had the same experience at the airport, but all who paid that extra fee eventually got their money back after arriving home.

It really felt great to be sitting on the plane when the time came to take off. The flight over to Johannesburg was direct but this time it went to Dakar, Senegal for a stopover of an hour and a half when some passengers departed. Several security men came on the plane to check things over, inspect all the empty seats and then sprayed; we weren't allowed to get off; then other passengers got on and we proceeded on our way. Each of the legs took about eight hours. We landed at Dulles and quickly went through immigration and passport control. I had about two hours free time before getting ready to board the plane to JFK for the first leg of my flight to SeaTac. That plane was more than an hour late taking off so I was a little concerned about meeting the next flight because I had only about an hour and fifteen minutes between flights. As it turned out, I had about five minutes to get to the next plane but luck was with me because the concourse where we disembarked was right next to the one I needed to go to, so everything went well. The Jet Blue flight from JFK was about six hours but the seats were comfortable and were wider than on any other economy seat configurations that I've been on.

The American versus foreign flights, as we've all come to know, are very different. In the former, one has to pay extra for any amenity, whereas in the latter, even on the smallest flights, the passengers are served a meal at no cost. On Jet Blue one can buy a blanket and pillow for $8.00 but "you can keep both when you leave", the flight attendant stated. How generous!

When I arrived at SeaTac, my whole family was there to meet me: Brad, Doug, Merrie, Racheal and a family friend, Paco. This was, indeed, a joyous occasion! When we drove up to my home, many yellow ribbons festooned the shrubbery and the front door. None of the family had done this nor the neighbors but I found out later that one of my good friends from church was the guilty party. When I went inside, my Christmas tree had been set up with other holiday decorations around the room; Granddaughter Racheal did this. All of this was exciting and a bit overwhelming on December 22, 2009 but I loved all of it!

So I came to the end of an unforgettable African adventure. I did enjoy it and learned a lot about the country of Namibia and its people as well as other places. I know that I gained much more than I gave. People at home have asked if I would like to go back and I reply, "No, I don't want to go back for another year to teach." I am happy that I did it and if I were younger I might consider it, but I like my life here, also. The year did go by quickly, especially the second half. I might consider a short term assignment if it really sounds interesting; I don't want to "close the door completely" to see more of the world. I would like to go back to Africa to visit because there is so much to see; I only saw a small part. I'll never forget those children/learners whom I taught and love and will wonder how they are getting along. I miss the staff at Heroes School and I miss my wonderful next door neighbors very much because they are the kindest most giving people that anyone could ever meet. They were especially helpful during my "broken patella" situation as were my friends, Evelyn and Chris. I did have a good situation there, better than some of my colleagues and I'm grateful for that. For several months after my return some people asked if I am well from the broken patella incident and I am. I don't even think about that anymore; I was very lucky with that by not having any residual effects after I was once healed. I'm grateful that I had the opportunity to travel during vacation times; this was the second reason I wanted to have this adventure. All in all it was a wonderful experience which I will always remember!

AFTERWARD

After returning from Namibia at the end of the 2009 year, I felt that I wanted to return to Ondangwa and Heroes School to visit the learners and staff whom I grew to know and love. This is going to come to fruition in late July of this year, 2011, when I go there. I will visit the village and school for a few days before I go to Moshi, Tanzania to volunteer in an orphanage for two months. I'm looking forward to this very much. It will be a different experience from Heroes but very rewarding, I'm sure. Once again, I know I will return home having received much more than I gave.

ABOUT THE AUTHOR

Helen Norene Harshbarger Hogle grew up living on small farms near West Milton, Ohio. She graduated from Miami University in Oxford, Ohio. Her career in education started with teaching in West Milton and Dayton, Ohio. Then she was with the Air Force Dependent Schools in Japan and England where she met her husband. He was from California and when they married they lived in the San Francisco Bay Area in Mountain View for thirty-four years. In 1967-68 they lived in American Samoa in an isolated village with their two young sons for one year where DeWitt was the principal of the school. When they returned to California they both taught school for a number of years there. After retiring they moved to the Puget Sound area of Washington where their sons had moved. Her husband and she wrote many accounts of the trips they were fortunate to take, but this is the first to be published by a "real" publisher.

Her husband died in 1998 but she continues to live in Mukilteo, WA and enjoys life. Her son, Brad, lives a few miles away and the other, Doug, lives with his wife, Merrie, about seventy miles to the north. Racheal lives up north, as well. Norene enjoys her retirement and has many interests including ballroom dancing, outdoor activities, music, being with friends and relatives and traveling to see other parts of the world.

APPENDICES

Namlish terms and meanings

Map of Africa

Map of Namibia

Namlish

Namlish	**English explanation**
How's it?	How are you doing?
How is the morning?	How are you?
It's **too** hot. She is **too** fat.	*Too* and *very* are interchangeable
How is the condition on your side?	How are you doing?
I'm coming now.	Said as one is leaving the room, meaning I'm coming right back.
Now	Not so much now. More like a while or maybe not at all.
Now now	Soon
Now now now	Now
Somehow	Can mean "just OK" as in "I'm feeling somehow" or not very smart as in, "That small boy is somehow."
Can I go with it?/Can you borrow me …	Can I borrow it? (You probably won't get it back.)

Help me dollar. Can you **help me** your stapler?	"Help me" is the polite way of asking for something.
Colleagues	Used to refer to peers, friends, coworkers
Let's push.	Come on. It's time to go.
We are/I am suffering.	There is some sort of a problem.
The time is going/running.	We are running out of time/you're wasting time/it's getting late.
I just came to visit you.	I want something, but I'm not going to tell you what it is until I waste at least a half hour of your time.
Are we together?	Is it clear? Are we on the same wave-length?
...and what what	...etcetera, etcetera.
Mmmmmm...	Yes
Cuca shop/Shebeen	An informal bar
Bakki	Pick-up truck
Combi/Kombi	large van type thing capable of holding a driver and 12 passengers plus babies
Cokey pens	Markers
Typex	White out
Rubber	Pencil eraser
Dustbin	Trash can
Rubbish	Trash
Robot	Traffic light
Trousers	Pants
Pants	Underwear
Cattle post	A place way out in the middle of nowhere where families with some level of wealth keep their cattle. Usually there is a small hut where the boys who are watching the cattle stay.
House	The homestead compound is called "house". All the huts are considered rooms in the "house".
Braai	Barbeque
Boerwoers	Sausage, typically thinner than a hotdog and darker in color
Hot stuff	Hard liquor
Lekker	Cool, great
/Na!	Cool
Bubbulas	Hung-over
Running stomach	Diarrhea

Footing	Walking
Soapie	Soap opera. Most of these are Mexican soap operas dubbed in English on NBC, shown right after the 8 PM news.

School-specific vocab:	**Definitions**
Learner	A student in grades k-12
Student	College or university student
Set/To set an exam	You make up (or copy) the questions. Teachers do this.
Write/To write an exam	You write the exam. Learners do this.
Exam	Big end-of-year or end-of-term test that determines their entire grade
Test	Any little test given during the term
Paper	Question paper=the exam/test itself
CASS marks	Continuous assessment marks=any marks given during the term on class work or homework
HIGCSE	Higher International General Certificate of Secondary Education
IGCSE	International General Certificate of Secondary Education
Scheme of work	What we call a syllabus. A detailed overview of what you will teach that year
Tuckshop	A little shop on the school premises where they sell pens, stamps, sweets, etc.
Text book	The book you are not supposed to write in, e.g. their English book or history book

Map of Africa

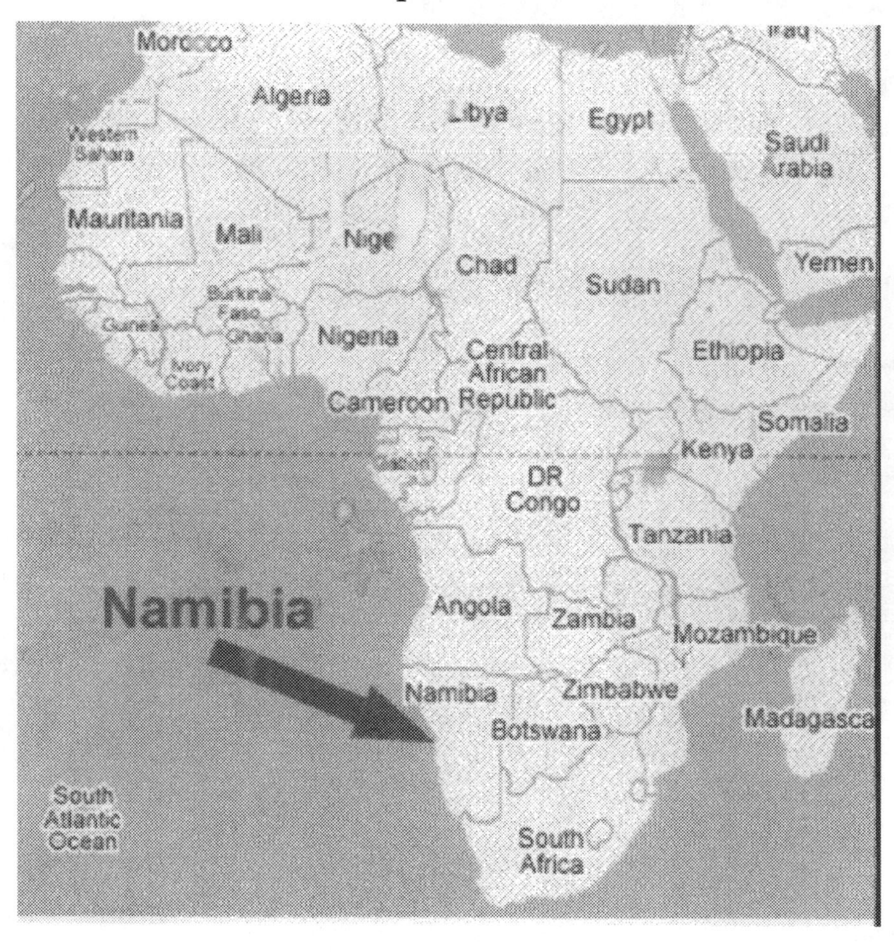

Map of Namibia

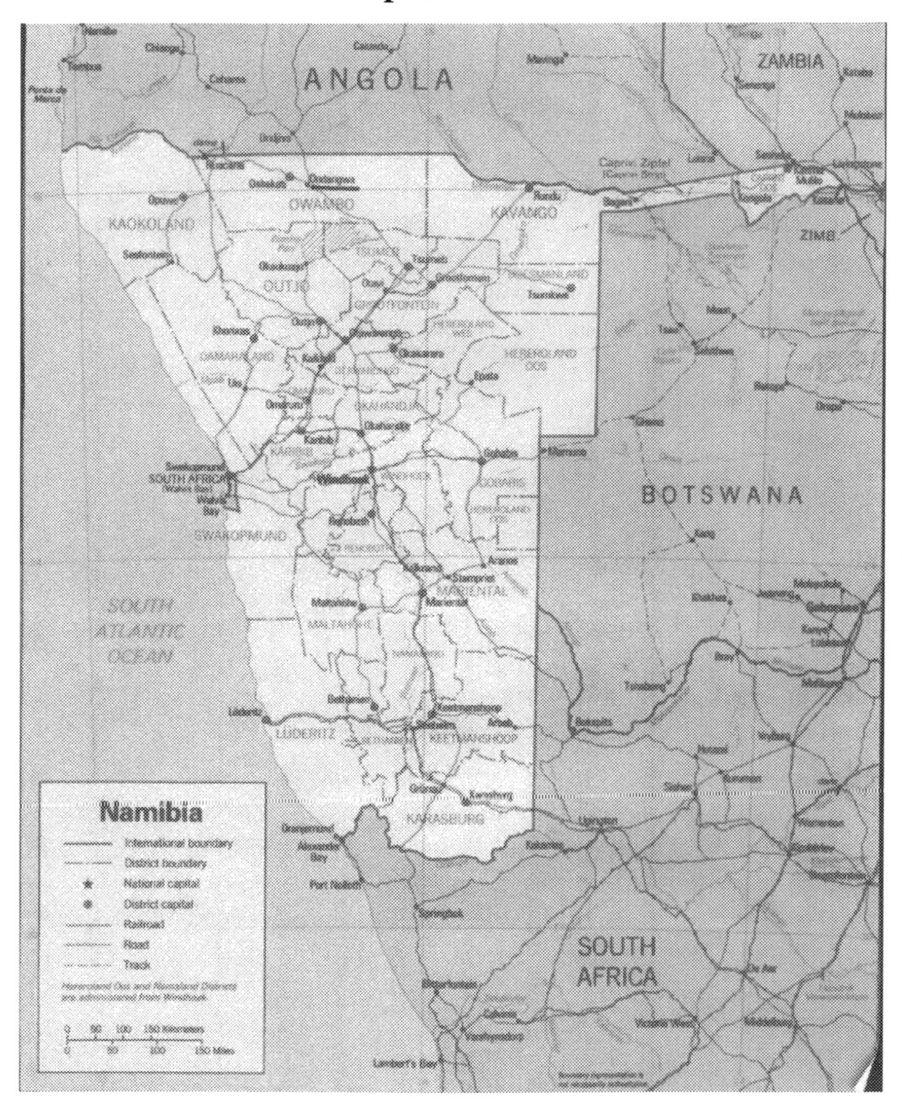